Acknowledgments:

I wanted to thank Allen, Graham, Allison, Johnson, and Yvonne for making this dream a reality. To every person who deals with discrimination and feels like no one else understands.

WEBSITE:

www.xanderbell.com

Material from Dr. Temple Grandin was given permission for use by Future Horizons Publication © 2011, 2012.

Table of Contents

CIRCUS RING #1

(LEFT RING)

Chapter 1: The Curtain Rises

"If there is no *fight*, there is no *change*."

Every staff member received a shirt with this quote printed on the back at J. Austen High School one year before the circus rolled into town. This quote eerily reflects my disturbing tale. The nerve-racking episodes I experienced set the stage for a real change and a fight forthcoming. Not the change I expected, but one that burned the brand of 'disability' on me. I need to be upfront and officially state that this story you will read literally happened, but, because of legal repercussions, I've had to alter every name and location of this story... but these events happened.

One can find the Jane Austen High School in Puzzle City, Michigan, home of the Knights! Just the sheer name of the school after the author, Jane Austen, is so ironic since she wrote magnificent works, and yet I would experience the very thing she tried to educate people about. If you weren't aware, she was the famous author of books such as *Pride and Prejudice* and *Sense and Sensibility*. Sadly, many of the so-called leaders of our school hadn't assimilated the whole message behind the classic literature.

 I have Asperger's Syndrome. Technically the condition is viewed as highly functional autism. The actual usage of the name is gradually being dropped and shoved under the full autism umbrella, but we're different from a person who is 'low functioning autistic'. A person with Asperger's has underdeveloped social skills and communication abilities. Some of us may have touch issues, disorganized thought processes or visual-spatial organizations, meaning we have trouble visually putting things into place. Because of our lack of communication skills, we'll be loners or be unwilling to take part in social functions. These are the obstacles I have every single day, whether I'm at work or home, it's a constant battle for control of me being able to function like any other normal human being.

I had to remind myself that I am blessed. Those words are a simple reminder that God is in control. I'm writing this book for two reasons: awareness and forgiveness. As our disorder of Asperger's Syndrome is gaining momentum in the public eye. One very glaring underlying issue with the Autism Spectrum Disorder or ASD which spreads throughout the workplace is what I call the Silent Discrimination. We've turned into a society where we yearn for equality and equitability with all races, sexual orientation, and gender in the job force. Yet, I've been a witness to a growing number of us who have this disorder and are having serious conflicts with employers. There is a huge divide between those of us with ASD just trying to do our jobs and the bosses who belittle those employees' efforts.

Just as anyone else, we want to live life, enjoy our time on this planet, work hard for our share, and make an impact. We truly commit ourselves to the job they gave us, but our 'awkwardness' draws negative attention. Thus, we display our tasks like we're not able to complete our duties in the eyes of our managers. Stuck in these uncomfortable conditions can make our workplaces appear as though it were a three-ring circus with us as the main event. The only way to break the Silent Discrimination of people with ASD requires education, understanding, and acceptance.

Since we have exposed a new revelation of the district's misconduct, I can now tell everyone the whole story of what happened to me and the Puzzle City Schools. We originally had an agreement where I withheld the harsh discriminatory information to myself in privacy. The school district pays me a specific sum of money and produces a neutral reference to any future employers who contact them referring to my preceding work experience. I discovered they fractured that agreement, so here's my story of how daunting it can be as an educator with Asperger's and the severe abuse I took from that district.

My wonderful wife and I were employed by The Puzzle City School District to which we served for several years. We were both proud to educate the students in the inner-city school system. Gaby embraced the initial excitement of teaching within the urban core. Sadly, Gaby had her own misfortune because of an injury and thus settled on a release from the district. I recognize this created a mixed sentiment in reflecting on her dream job and the tragedy that fell on her.

Allow me to start with the proper setting for the beginning of the greatest show on earth. I began teaching for the Puzzle City Schools in August 1996. Since that time, I moved around to a few of the different schools before I ended up at Jane Austen High School (or JAHS) in 2005. During that year, the school moved through absolute chaos because the district had decided to close Green High School and combine their students with those of J. Austen.

That infamous decision led to the changing of principals three times in one school year, a huge increase in security, and lots of false alarm calls that cost the district thousands of dollars. I taught middle school social studies because superintendent Dr. J. Dollar put 7th and 8th-grade students in with high school students. When I entered the building for the first time, I recognized there were two things I needed urgently: to rejoin the union — AFT (American Federation of Teachers), and to put into place by the American Disabilities Act (ADA) accommodations.

As for the workplace ADA accommodations, the diagnosis of Asperger's Syndrome became official back in the summer of 1999, so my wife told me I needed to go into Human Resources and fill out a job-accommodation questionnaire. After Gaby and I filled out the form and gave it back, HR reviewed the information, approved it, placed it in my file, and then informed the school administration of my needs so I could do my job properly and without bias. Sadly, the person in charge of my accommodations never got it past the review part of the refining. My accommodations remained a secret from Human Resources until it was far too late.

These were my agreed-upon accommodations:

- Remove or reduce distractions from my classroom.
- Supply proper working equipment and office supplies.
- Give specific feedback to help employee (myself) target areas of improvement. (This is possible with my disability.)
- Prepare written instructions or general information. This includes a written transcription of meeting notes or use a recording device.
- Prompt me with verbal cues.
- Allow increasing training time for new tasks. (if I consider it's needed)
- Pinpoint areas of improvement for the employee in a fair and consistent manner.
- Give adequate notice of any changes in the regular workday or any meetings. (This included any person wanting to enter the classroom for any reason because this ties into the first accommodation.)

My first year in J. Austen High was one I wanted to forget because that was the year of the great Green/JAHS high school merging that turned our school into a huge flea circus. That was one of the craziest school years I had ever experienced. When I first started, they placed me with high school students and I was pretty excited because this was the first time I would get to teach a new subject to students. To my irritation, they moved me to middle school because I lacked a high school license to teach social studies, and I tried to plead my case that we were already halfway through the school year. Suddenly, I got stuck teaching 7th and 8th graders and I hated it. The behavior got so bad that I got some disturbing news on April 11th of 2007. The third and last principal that year sent me an email with a warning:

Xander,

The librarian shared with me that students reported you as a target of the teacher "jump day." As a result, I have asked the officer to come to speak with you personally.

He will share the following with you: If you have been threatened and/or uncomfortable, I am happy to relieve you of your duties today and you can work in the main office. Please give me notice if this course of action is your wish.

In the meantime, I have then alerted the PCPD and the Central Office Administration. I have likewise directed the security team to be in your vicinity during passing periods. We then have an increasing hallway presence on every floor.

I need you to alert me if there is anything more I can do.

(Principal from 2006 to 2007 school year)

Yes, I took the principal up on his offer. I was already becoming a nervous wreck, and this plight did not help. After the threat, I suspect that was when my doctor permanently pulled me from the classroom for the rest of the year because I was seriously being overtaxed on my mental state. The stress was so rough, my left Trapezius muscle would tighten up, and I had to have physical therapy to loosen the muscle. This didn't happen just once... it happened at the end of my last year as well — yes, the condition was that stressful! This was the point where I became angry with the AFT because I received no help or advice that the school year from my union.

During the second year, there were several changes where the district removed many of the students from the building, and we now had a strong core of teachers and a brand-new set of administrators. The new principal was Dr. E. Strongman, and I still have the greatest respect for his vision and leadership. Thus, the 2006-2007 and 2007-2008 school years were major turnarounds for J. Austen High. I can say this about the Puzzle School District: when something is going absolutely well, upper leadership will ultimately tear it apart.

Tearing down concepts that help any school always seems to be a pattern they follow to the letter. I will illustrate the entire series of deliberate mismanagement of the district and why I ultimately became a target just by questioning their motives. To give you a good idea of what I'm referring to, a great example would be a time when the school had a special program set up between the University of Michigan-Puzzle City (UMPC) and the W. William's foundation, where students took classes with state colleges or had teachers within the high school teaching courses for college credit.

One day, out of the blue, the Puzzle City school district decided the program was a waste of money, stopped the funding and abruptly ceased the whole program before the end of the school year. The sad part was that I was one of those teachers who got chosen to take college classes to teach college courses for UMPC. I was a volunteer college professor where I didn't receive a salary from the university, but I was still a representative. My title was to be an adjunct professor. (I still receive ROBO calls from the university on different emergency alerts on campus... weird.) This was a moment that started making me question our leadership for the district, the inquiry that finally got me sunk. Since they destroyed the program, a few administrators left because of the debacle.

We were on the verge of rolling into my final year with Puzzle City Public Schools, 2009-2010. Call this an omen, but an accident that was about to happen to me. This shouldn't have been a surprise, but it's true. Before school started, they usually gave teachers preparation time to get their classrooms ready. On the first Monday back, I was an idiot and stood on top of a student desk to fix a blind. I stuck out a coat hanger to adjust the blind when suddenly the desk started to wobble. I sensed the desk give away, and I lost my balance. As the desk tipped over, I fell on the back of a nearby chair and broke two of my ribs. If you've never had the experience of breaking your ribs, then let me just say, one: never let it happen to you, and two: it will hurt to breathe — a lot.

Once school started, I still had trouble breathing because of my injury, and to make things worse, I received news that wasn't very pleasant. The students tested horrible last year on the End Of Course exams. Their scores were so atrocious that our school placed last on the American Government part of the state test compared to the other Puzzle City schools. In complete fairness, the year before was the first time I'd ever taught American Government, and I never got the training to help these students be successful for the test.

With this last place showing, I had the pleasure of getting bombarded from literally every single administrator and my Social Studies coordinator in the first week of class! I'm sure the first question here would be 'Did they just violate one of my accommodations?' and the answer is yes. The visits weren't rough, however; my leaders wanted to make sure we got off to a better start than we did last year. This leads to the question of 'where were you last year?!' After the 'visits', I was still not getting the help I needed from the AFT union, so on August 31 of that year, I changed unions. I needed a union that was not afraid of the PC school district and would annoy any administrator who chose not to treat me properly.

The National Education Association (NEA) was not the negotiating union with the school district, but I still had a right to have them as my representation. It was a good thing I made the change, because after my visit from the administrators, on September 4th, Vice-Principal Ms. S. Puppet wanted to put me on a Professional Growth Plan (PGP). For those of you who are not privy to what a PGP is, it's basically the beginning stages of trying to get you fired. The proper statement is that they use a PGP to help aid a teacher in developing proper guidance to help them educate students. Now mind you, we're not speaking of a self-designed program; it's more to the effect of a Professional Gotcha' Plan. If you don't believe me, let me quote how the district describes what is to happen with a PGP:

"The performance improvement process should begin before they implement a PGP through informal observations, conferences, individual development strategies, and coaching conversations. A professional growth plan should not come as a surprise to the educators involved."

The irony is that they used this program to help struggling *new* teachers, and this was my 18th year of teaching. Yes, it did "come as a surprise." The PGP just added to the stress level and didn't focus on the real problem: a lack of parental involvement when student state scores were low. I signed the plan off on September 20th, 2009, just over a month after school started that year. I absolutely didn't want to sign the PGP, but my union told me I didn't have a choice. So, in the preceding days of September 30th, October 1st and October 9th, I received observations in my classes with no 'adequate notice'. This PGP was doing a good job of frustrating me because I needed to focus on the students. Instead, I was constantly looking out for Ms. Puppet.

At the end of the first quarter, my union rep and I sat down with my principal Dr. Strongman and the VP Ms. Puppet. During the meeting, the administrators thought I was doing well. They left me wondering who gave the order to put me on this PGP if my principal figured I was doing my job. My union rep met with my principal privately to inform him about the possibility of my moving to a different school if it came to it, but Dr. Strongman sounded as though that shouldn't be necessary. I had a PGP review on October 29th and my vice-principal stated, "Since they put the initial PGP into place, I have been into Mr. Bell's room again and again with the last visit being October 21, 2009."

I was so exhausted from the mountain of observations I didn't even record the Oct. 21 visit in my personal journal. Even though my review progressed well, the vice-principal stated something toward the end of the review that undoubtedly made me mad. Here is what she said, "*Overall there has been marked improvement with Mr. Bell's classroom observations. I see continual monitoring through the end of the school year will make sure these improvements continue...*" I still remember "*through the end of the school year*" just burning into my skull! I suffered like a rotten dog looped up on a choke leash and a cone wrapped around my neck... are you kidding me?!!!

The month of November was quiet. I received a visit on November 16th from the principal, a vice-principal, handful representatives from the Department of Elementary and Secondary Education (DESE) and the head of Secondary Education for the district Mr. K. Tamer. I learned they were in the building that day, but I didn't realize that they were coming to my room. Mr. Tamer and his team took a moment to look around the room and thanked me when they left. I literally had to stop because no teaching happened with the unwanted commotion. The visit unnerved the students. I realized these visits were taking their toll. The best way to describe how I comprehended things when I had a visitor was like this: You're watching your favorite show live and suddenly someone calls for you in the next room and you end up missing the most important part of the show.

One would consider December to be a month full of good tidings and great joy. Sadly, this didn't happen. I learned that a fellow teacher friend of both my wife and I was forced to leave at the end of the semester. I had a feeling the administration would finally get to my friend. He had been teaching for a great extent of time and he earned a doctorate in his field of teaching, but that didn't save him.

My vice-principal did one last observation for the year on Dec. 18th. They labeled the official visit as 'formal', but just like with several before this, this was informal and unannounced. I mean surely why change it up now? The comments on the visit were lukewarm. The vice-principal had checked most of the areas of my instruction as 'developing'. The only section I received a 'needs improvement' was for classroom management. The vice principal's idea of "management" was "integrating rigorous instruction and engaging activities" so the problem was two-fold. I restrained from locking my door and the hall outside my door was constantly being disrupted by several students in the hallway! And remember, any teacher's union will tell you 'never touch a student or block the door'; I understand the safety behind the warnings, but this made the 'management' even more difficult.

To put the cherry on top, in the same month, Dr. Strongman had pulled me aside on the last day before Christmas break to tell me that none of my Government students who took the End Of Course exams just before the end of the semester, scored in the Proficient section and roughly half of them were Basic or Below Basic which to say the news was considerably frustrating didn't say it enough. If you thought the first half of this school year was interesting and infuriating, just wait until you read what happens in the second half. I recognize you'll wonder how the hell did I ever even keep my sanity together... Merry Christmas!

We ushered in 2010 and we had a hard time getting school started because of snow days. The circus tent was rising up and the show was about to begin. They left me relatively alone for the first couple of weeks in January, but the real fun was just about to begin.

The infamous week started on January 18th when we celebrated Martin Luther King Jr.'s birthday. I remember the incredible irony that here we were remembering what Martin Luther King did for the equal rights of every race of people, and here I was on the threshold of having to defend myself from the prejudices of my own Autistic condition. I began to understand how difficult it must have been for Dr. King to cry out for equality when most people were not willing to listen.

On Tuesday the 19th, I met with my Social Study Coordinator, Ms. A. Juggler to help rewrite the mock EOC test. I will further explain what I mean. The district wanted to get an idea of how students might do on the actual EOC test. As a gauge, they gave a mock state test in every school subject. When I gave the test, every student in my class failed and I recognized why. When I looked at the test, I noticed several issues with missing answers to questions, answers that didn't fit the question, and answers with no question. Since my coordinator used to teach in the same building and we had a mutual understanding of one another, she wanted me to report to the education center and help rewrite the test so we might get a more authentic score. Sadly, this information did not get back to the top brass before my big meeting the next day.

The date that changed everything was Wednesday, January 20th. Here was the email I received dated January 19th:

Good Afternoon,

Just a reminder, you will meet with me to discuss your data tomorrow morning. We will be joined in the Conference Room next to my office, by (Instructional Coach), Dr. S. Ringmaster, and 3 others from the BOE (Board of Education). Be prepared to speak to your data and discuss your plan to drive student achievement. You need to take along any data to help discuss our plan for success.

If you are unsure, the Puzzle City District-Wide Strategies are: Increasing Student Engagement, Increasing the Effectiveness of Data Teams, and Implementing a Literacy Plan (consider your use of close reading strategies, note-taking & summarizing, inference and drawing conclusions as they pertain to your subject- and remember, WE ARE ALL READING TEACHERS.)

Don't be nervous. If you are, just try to focus on having a conversation with me. During the data consults last week, everyone seemed to have a plan to move forward — we just need to move forward with the plan.

Respectfully,

Dr. E. Strongman

I perceived this meeting would take place. I didn't get a lot of details, but I learned that the superintendent was sending groups around different schools. Their job was to find out why the district was having a hard time getting better scores in order to meet one requirement from the State Board of Education for accreditation. For a short time, the Puzzle City School District had their school accreditation removed by the State of Michigan because of several issues the district had, including test scores.

I realized that my Social Studies coordinator, Ms. Juggler was one person chosen to lead one group. The reason I say this about Ms. Juggler is to show that they made up her group with different people from the central office. I recognized that Dr. Ringmaster and his band of circus performers preferred not to have been in her group. So, I promise you, I honestly wished her group had come to my school because I had no doubt my whole incident would have had a completely different result.

I had received the email earlier that morning, with the tagline "Data Meeting", and they scheduled it for 10:00 that morning. I was teaching a class when I got the call to make the long walk to the office, so I had a substitute come to relieve me. As I made the journey, I tried to remember helpful ideas I wanted to say to the team and what Dr. Strongman had instructed me to say. He instructed me to have him present most of the discussion and just answer any of the team's questions. The data team would want to hear how we were using reading in our classes and anything 'Marzano'.

Before I continue, I must explain 'Marzano'. Robert Marzano is an education researcher and developer of the method of teaching that several school districts have adopted. Marzano has a few good tips for teachers but, for complete intents and purposes, he just took old teaching method terms and renamed them to make it his own 'educational philosophy' and program.

As I arrived at the conference room, I prayed a small prayer, not knowing what to expect on the other side. I mean, since I never received my pre-set questions or at least an agenda for the meeting, I found myself at a severe disadvantage.

The spotlights got completely set, and the show was ready to begin. I entered the conference arena and faced the whole cast of characters sitting there trying to look important. Dr. E. Strongman showed me to my seat and the main event began. Each person introduced themselves. I presumed they started to my left with Dr. Strongman. After him was Mr. T. Tightrope, who was in charge of technology for the whole district, then it was Mr. K. Tamer who was head of secondary education. Dr. S. Ringmaster sat straight across from me, which virtually appeared as one of those wild west showdowns.

Then continuing was Dr. E. Fire-Eater who was the head of elementary and secondary education, followed by Ms. T. Audience who was the director of student support and neighborhood service. Finally, there was Ms. V. Acrobat who was the district's chief academic and accountability officer. Dr. Strongman opens the discussion by explaining how I was using reading within my class to help improve test scores. He said that since this was only my second year teaching upper-level students, I was still trying to figure out what method was the right tool to use to help students succeed. The committee acknowledged that my test scores had improved, but the discussion traveled south in a hurry.

Mr. Tamer mentioned several times that my American government students were testing 93% below basic. I tried to advise the committee that the tests had several flaws and were not a proper measure of our student's knowledge. Dr. Fire-Eater had a twist in her perspective regarding my classes, and she said, with a high cackling sound, "What you have, Mr. Bell, is a five-alarm fire in your room!"

Her 'educational observation' threw me back. I tried to remind them that my Social Studies coordinator and I had been trying to fix the defective mock EOC test. If the almighty central office members had mentioned the poor American government test scores, I honestly don't recall. I was fed up with their nonsense. They weren't listening to a single word Dr. Strongman or I had to say.

I then remembered two things I needed to say to them. When the moment finally came, I asked Dr. Ringmaster about the laptop program, which was that every student would receive a laptop computer, but the mention of the failed program drew a very sharp look directly at the head of technology. I instantly could tell that I had just stepped on a raw nerve. The tech guy, Mr. Tightrope, told me that there was a slight delay, but they hoped to have something in place soon. I called this the best correct response you might give because Dr. Ringmaster had been hoping for the last couple of years that every student would have those said laptops.

My last comment was for Dr. Ringmaster alone. I had been so frustrated by all my government classes because my students were not using the tools I gave them. I gave them note cards to help them understand what the question on the EOC was asking of them. I recognized that if they can understand the terms used on the test, then they should have a much higher chance of selecting the correct answer. My frustration was when students had their note cards to review, they elected not to review them. I remember calling the parents of all my students and begging them to please remind their child to look at the note cards. Still no improvement. I asked them every single day I saw them. Nothing. This was the result I kept getting — nothing.

So, with that little backstory in mind, I looked at Dr. Ringmaster square in the face and told him: "The biggest issue we as teachers are having is that school isn't going home."

Dr. Ringmaster nodded, responded with a very simple thank you, and that was the end of the meeting. To say they upset me was light-years from the truth; it made me furious. Whether my showdown with the superintendent was brave or foolhardy, I will leave to the court of public opinion. I'm a teacher, I relate with my students, so to sit in that joke of a discussion and have them being ridiculed for playing around, not being focused or prepared, wasn't fair. In my mind, I never considered I might have just jeopardized my educational career in that meeting; I saw that I finally got the chance to articulate my opinions to people that could make a real change if they wanted to see improvements. I'll consider it safe to say improvements are one thing that leadership didn't care much about, because rumors had been swirling that the state of Michigan was seriously considering taking over the school district, so 'higher-up' jobs might have been on the line. Whatever the reason, the leadership didn't seem to care about anything about the staff or the students.

The last part of January and the entire month of February sounded relatively quiet. As a parent, if there is one thing I've learned with kids, it's that if your house suddenly goes quiet it means that, whatever the children got into never ends well. The same applied to my workplace. When all was quiet, it meant that trouble was brewing. The Puzzle City School District, as I learned later, was prepping for a true downright nasty plot, planning out my future demise with them, but I was not privy to their plan. The only thing that happened between the end of January and the beginning of March was that I received a peculiar visit from an odd fellow. I was progressing through my business by introducing the lesson to the students. The students were ready for the World War I lesson since their knowledge on this topic was limited. I was just as excited because this was a war that was losing its importance in our American History.

The environment outside was crisp since we were talking wintertime in Michigan; at least the rooms were still warm. But that morning, my classroom door flew open, introducing the breeze of cooler air from the hallway. I was on the receiving end of a visit from a very unusual gentleman who had pranced in. I gazed at him with a look of complete bewilderment on my face. The man was bald with thick black square-rimmed glasses, sporting a suit, and a heavy black suit coat. The eccentric man had a scent of expensive cologne, but I suddenly had a sickening sensation in my stomach that he wasn't here for myself or the students' gain. He hovered around the room, looking like an apparition.

Right behind the floating entity was his handler in the form of my Instructional Coach, but the weird part was I had no knowledge I'd be receiving a visit, and in what undoubtedly showed to be considerably unprofessional, the coach didn't even introduce me to the mysterious man! As he loomed around my class, my students and me, he created a series of perplexing looks. I quickly scanned the room to see how my kids were handling this disruption of their learning time, and my students' looks were the same as mine: irritation, disrespect, and a complete buzzkill. When the man finally floated out like Mary Poppins, a genuinely aggravated student piped up a question I had earlier formed in my head. "Hey, Mr. Bell. Who the hell was that?" I just shrugged my shoulders and responded with, "Your guess is as good as mine."

Later, I learned that the person was Mr. A. Big-Top who was the Chief Financial Officer. Mr. Big-Top was the Number Two person in the district. I'm not entirely sure why he was compelled to visit or why my coach neglected to even introduce the man to me but, I suspected that the first shot was just fired.

Chapter 2: The Scene Change

March came in with a spine-tingling lion act from the circus. The unannounced vice-principal visits started up again, but this time with a dark, unexpected twist. The VP came into my third-period class, which was a better class for me. Unlike the improving reports I had been receiving up to the Christmas break, this one hit me hard like a pie to the face.

This was the beginning comments to her observation: "There were five students with their electronic devices out and I noted two with their heads down on the desk at various times during my visit. (Meaning, I kept having to wake them up and pay attention.) There was likewise one student with her back to the classroom as she was facing the wall. (Because she personally hated Ms. S. Puppet.) There were nineteen students present, and it involved relatively five of them in the discussions and answering the questions. The rest of the class, although quiet, was not engaged in the material." (Hinting, not answering my questions.)

Very different from my observations before Winter Break. The VP states that I had never addressed the students with their cell phones or the ones with their heads dropped... even though she observed that their head was up and down. As you can see, the VP was getting desperate for any issues. She was trying her best to find the worst stuff possible and having a hard time doing it. The only real way she could get any information was literally observing outside my classroom from the 5th period all the way to the 7th period. This was her observation:

"On Tuesday, March 2nd, between hours 5-7, I observed no less than three students per hour walking in or out of his room."

 Two of the students disclosed where they were going. They told me they moved in there to get their things because they didn't want to carry them around the school, but students didn't have lockers. When I sat down with Ms. Puppet and she ran over the points of her observation, I identified immediately something had changed and it wasn't good. With the vice-principal trying to find as much negative material as possible, I realized a meeting with my NEA rep should happen soon with the entire negative observations.

On Friday, March 5th, my NEA rep and I met at a Starbucks in downtown Puzzle City, where we mainly addressed the sudden issues different from last week. The rep wanted to go over everything she learned at the time and she gave me direct instructions. I've included below the email my rep sent to my wife describing our meeting:

Good evening, Xander & Gaby -

As promised, I wanted to send a summary of the conversation Xander and I had yesterday afternoon at Starbucks.

My big goal in sending this summary to you, Gaby, where you feel confident that you are with me on the same mission. Since I understand that Xander might get easily distracted while recounting a verbal discussion, so I'm giving Xander a checkpoint he can refer back to if he finds himself confused where things stand on his employment.

(1) The first thing Xander and I discussed was the Wednesday meeting with Dr. Strongman and Ms. Puppet. Xander had sent me an email over his work account voicing anger over this meeting, the district's failure to follow his ADA accommodations, and his frustration over the poor job critiques. Xander again voiced a need to realize and assured that I am on your team as a family and on Xander's team as an employee of Puzzle City, Michigan.

I told Xander that I regretted not getting back to him at once. I had internal work issues fall on my lap following our meeting with Dr. Strongman and the vice-principal Ms. Puppet that delayed my response. I shared my honest feelings with regard to the meeting. They threw me off guard by the discussion. I saw when we arrived the conversion rang a distinctly different tone and intent than all the prior meetings we had about his PGP. Since early fall, as you both know, Xander's PGP meetings have been an annoyance for him but have not resulted in burdensome outcomes. There has been no increase in demand from the district or claims that Xander has failed those PGP guidelines that applied to him.

I informed Xander that I was able to understand his frustration expressed in his email. I had not been an attack dog against Ms. Puppet and Dr. Strongman. I tried to share my thoughts on my concerns to the administration and to back up Xander's accommodations. We need to play it safe because something serious had shifted with his administrators and I didn't realize what I was dealing with concerning the change of plans. {Early on, Ms. Puppet had implied that Ms. A. Warrior was rather aggressive based on the VP's observations, so she referred to Ms. Warrior as an "attack dog." What Ms. Puppet didn't understand was that it still based these early observations on my PGP that started off the school year, which, in the eyes of the NEA, was an aggressive move on the school's part.}

(2) Convo [conversions] with Dr. Strongman. I told Xander that I had an appointment to have a one on one with Dr. Strongman yesterday. We discussed my problems with the Wednesday meeting now that I had the time and space to ponder on the matter and come to a decisive conclusion.

In this conversation, I realize Dr. Strongman was honest and upfront with me. He shared that yes, things had shifted on their end. My assumption from both Xander and myself was correct. He sounded regretful of this but he shared that recently. The superintendent himself had voiced concerns about Xander regarding a meeting we had in which showed his lack of clarity when asked to discuss the Marzano teaching strategies. My take on what Dr. Strongman was saying, look, 'my' boss is telling me he's not happy with Xander Bell. We're happy with Xander, but I have to follow orders. That's why the meeting which scrutinized Xander as a teacher had a different tone this week. {We believe Dr. Ringmaster had sent Mr. Big-Top in my room to see for himself what was the concern.}

(3) After hearing this I started to argue considering Xander's disability and how any judgment made by the superintendent. He solely based on what he saw and ignorantly based on no information or understanding of Xander's struggles. Dr. Strongman concurred and promptly we came to the agreement that Xander is a valuable member of the Puzzle City, Michigan district, that Jane Austen High School is far too stressful a placement for him respecting his needs for support to be healthy. Dr. Strongman wanted to work with me (us) to help Xander land via transfer at a better teaching assignment.

I shared with Xander that having his principal behind us in the effort to transfer was precious. At the end of our meeting, Dr. Strongman linked me up with the head of HR [Dr. M. Clown], another influence for us since Dr. Strongman himself was endorsing my goals (Xander Bell) in connecting Dr. Clown and me to arrange for a meeting concerning Xander's future with PCPS.

I explained to Xander that I had emailed Dr. Clown to follow up on Dr. Strongman's email and that I hadn't heard as of Friday (email sent the same day). As of Saturday night, I still have not heard but my goal is to meet with her to begin discussions of Xander's transfer at the end of the year ASAP.

(4) Xander and I discussed "no more venting" over school email accounts and a general clean manner needs to be our strategies while heading back to work. I told Xander that I will follow back up with Dr. Strongman after the meeting with Dr. Clown to confront the stressful issues of the PGP/work out an agreement that their scrutiny must stop because of Xander's limited future at JAHS.

I discussed with Xander the need to come to Jane Austen High School to examine his classroom as a strategic step to let Dr. Strongman and the vice-principal "off the hook" for the PGP. Every issue still needs straightening out based on what results come from my meeting with Dr. Clown. I am committed to trying to focus on the current work environment stress that is pushing Xander to the limit of his health.

(5) Xander and I debated transfer options, what he is and is not interested in for choices of schools. Xander agreed to finish his transfer application within the Puzzle City, Michigan internet database by Monday so that Dr. Clown can pull his file when we meet.

(6) Xander and I discussed my perceptions of our work together up to this point. That, without trying to bring false security to the future, I thought our work to this point to be very successful considering the legal limits which we've had to use. That my big goal for Xander this year has been stability. We backed the vice-principal off the PGP in early fall - and while annoying - his health had been in a stable place through the first semester versus what scenarios we easily might have been dealing with the hostility now in play. I reminded Xander that we have zero legal arguments concerning why they placed him on a PGP and whether the decision was legitimate — that administrators in Michigan can use this willy-nilly whenever, wherever, and for as long as they so choose. We've done well on this stage. I have dozens of teachers who are forced to do more and more demands at every single PGP meeting, for example.

I further discussed how the district's changed position this week meant we were at go time. I encouraged Xander to hold his strength and constitution so he didn't hit meltdown mode before we got to his goals, to play it cool so to speak. He agreed to let me do the fighting for him and he said he understood that my strategy might look less confrontational but justified (i.e., working internally for a transfer). My dealing with the conflict was better than a bloody fight because your family had been through that with Gaby [she had her own legal issue with the district] and had not seen a very satisfying reward (as is 99% the case versus more stealth/behind the scenes work).

(7) Xander agreed he shall get me copies of his ADA accommodation paperwork and said he should have you, Gaby, write up a short road map of your litigation experience with the school district. The reason I requested this won't be relevant now, but, if Xander's future does not pan out per our goals and we are looking at legal action relating to the district's failure to follow the law on his disability. It may be helpful to have a sense of what their policy is regarding being sued by employees. i.e., if they settle, when, and for what expense versus what is being sought.

Ok, guys, that's it. I am following up with you as soon as I hear from Dr. Clown and that's our next concrete step.

Text/call if you have questions and thanks for your patience.

• My NEA Representative Ms. A. Warrior

Before I continue, I need to mention that my wife, Gaby had her own legal battle with the district and settled. Because of the legality of her case, I don't believe I'm able to speak on it, but I can on mine! Ms. Warrior had a bunch of hard truths to tell me and I needed it. The plan was to transfer out of the school and hoping that might be the end... we were genuinely holding fast to Dr. Strongman. The rep and I presumed he held the power to make the transfer happen. One other note, this will be the first time I mentioned Dr. Clown who was the temporary head of Human Resources. She will play a more prominent role later on in this tale. Dr. Clown is the person through which the school transfer was supposed to happen.

Similar to the eye of a hurricane, Spring Break fell upon the school district and I was very delighted to see it. I was truly getting sick of this observation Merry-Go-Round. Spring Break fell on March 15 through the 19th. The only dangerous part regarding the eye of the hurricane is that once it passes, you get the storm again! I recall trying my very best to enjoy the time off, but that was difficult with the complete craziness happening at work. They set a meeting between my rep Ms. Warrior and Dr. Clown during the break, but that meeting never happened.

As the Ides of March in Julius Caesar, my Lunar March was on March 26th. The meeting that my NEA rep was looking for ended up being a meeting at school that Friday morning. In an exchange of emails earlier in the week, my rep had asked Dr. Clown, "I am not sure I understand the purpose of our meeting

Friday, to be honest. Trying to help Xander prepare - can you share a bit of insight?"

Dr. Clown responded to my rep's email just over an hour later, "Yes, I want to understand what accommodations he trusts he needs to have to be successful and engage in a conversation about what we can and cannot reasonably do."

The rep Ms. Warrior shared this information with me and told me, "Xander, my impression is that this meeting is in response to my raising hell last week regarding their not having your accommodations on file." (To which I need to explain):

If there was one thing I've learned with the Puzzle City Public Schools, it's that they love to throw people off their own true intentions. The district always kept people guessing on their plans. This nonsense of not having my accommodations on record was... a lie. Surprised? The reason they were telling my rep that they didn't have the accommodations was to stall them until the end of the week. The district was trying to distract my rep and stall the communication to buy extra time so they may not meet any other day but Friday.

The head of HR might have still been getting her orders and didn't want to share that information with my rep, but Dr. Clown made sure every player was there during the morning meeting at the school. That morning, March 26th, myself, my rep, Dr.

Strongman, and Dr. Clown sat down, and Dr. Clown told us what my options were: No school transfer — I could either take a paid administrative leave, quit and find another job, or stay and be terminated. The only thing I can tell you is that my instant reaction was a sheer sinking in my stomach because none of those options sounded favorable, which I was not expecting. I didn't know what to think. What the heck did I do wrong to warrant this extreme final decision?

Too many emotions were swarming in my head all at once. They gave me two days to consider my choice, and that was the point of no return. No discussion of accommodations, no talk of moving to a different school, just her explicit instructions from the top people to (as the head of HR put it to my NEA rep Ms. Warrior later in April) *"**get rid of the weirdo**"*. Those were the orders of the leadership of the Puzzle City School District... throw out the weirdo. Fourteen years. For fourteen years, I served as an educator for one of the largest school districts in the city, and this discriminatory decision is how the district wanted to see my career end. My wife and I had a difficult life-changing decision to make.

A little irony — in an email Dr. M. Clown responded to a comment I had made about making sure she understood my accommodations since she was new, and she wrote this back on Apr 1st: "Thank You for letting me know. I comprehend your accommodation requests. That was the reason I came to see you personally on March 26, 2010, to review what accommodations you needed and to talk about how we might best serve your needs." [As you just read... that didn't happen.]

I realize that we as humans have this fight-or-flight instinct in every one of us. Gaby and I debated on what decision to make. I admit there was a part of me that wanted to end this. Realize that with my Asperger's Syndrome, I'm not too fond of confrontations. I try hard to avoid any conflict because I hate having my nerves rattled. I recognize my wife agonized over my position because she didn't want to see me go through what will be an unrelenting time if I'd return, however; she wanted to see me fight this to the end. In my exchanges with my NEA rep, I was pondering about getting my resume together and seeing if I could get another job quicker, so my leaving the district would make my life easier. My rep wanted to preserve both options and get back to us on what to do; however, we didn't have much time. So remembering the raw deal my wife had received with the district in her case, we dug in our heels and on April 1st, April Fool's day (LOTS of ironies there!) I emailed Dr. Clown and told her I'd be reporting back to work the next day.

At the start of the meeting, they told me my options, what would happen if I stayed, and they'd place me on a NOD or Notice of Deficiency, which meant observations will blast in hot and heavy. On the morning of April 2nd, I remember walking into Dr. Strongman's office and in there was a black gentleman I had never seen before, and wondered if he was a higher-up person from the district. I recall Dr. Strongman telling me that this was Mr. D. Magician of the leadership team, and he was here for another matter. I first determined when I met him that he had a smug look about him, but I didn't give it much of a concern because I realized why I was in his office... the signing of the NOD. In theory, when a teacher works under a PGP, if they have poorly performed the set requirements they signed off for and showed no professional growth with their objectives, then a Notice of Deficiency activates. The NOD is a document for serving notice that the teacher needs to improve or risk termination. (You realize the district did not use any of the plans the way it meant to be used. And... April 2nd of every year is World Autism Awareness Day. I guess the district missed that memo.)

As I sat there with Dr. Strongman looking over the NOD, my brain was translating the plan as... well... "Blah, blah, blah, blah, blah." The district set several dates for 'formal' observations and reserved the right for any volume of informal observations and walkthroughs at any point. You need to realize that I put 'formal' in quotes because one of the ADA accommodations was that ANY observation must have 24-hour notice. They mentioned no accommodations in the NOD, so I'm sure you can guess how this went down. I will mention the complete dates listed on the NOD as a reference when I describe the relentless pressure I was about to confront: Apr. 5, Apr. 7, Apr. 9, Apr. 14, Apr. 16, Apr. 21, Apr. 23, Apr. 28, Apr. 30, May 5, and May 7.

After the meeting, I stood up and shook Dr. Strongman's hand, but little did I know that this will be the last time I would see him again. My classroom environment will change, and I had no clue what was to come.

On Tuesday, April 6th, an emergency meeting processed that morning before school, so the entire faculty and staff had to report to the library. Settling down, I couldn't guess what this impromptu sideshow was about this time, and you understand by now that J. Austen HS definitely had its share of many issues.

To give you some background story, we've tried hard to hold the fort down in the school considering the chaos we had to endure just a few years prior. Sadly, we had been having too many problems that were not Dr. Strongman's fault. He might have been the principal, but when the district didn't give him any freedom to make good sound decisions to improve the school, there was the chance things could end badly, of which the onset was when the first sexual assault case happened earlier that same school year.

A few examples of the things he tried to get were cameras, yes... cameras. The school didn't have any except out on the exterior of the building! Another needed priority was more security guards. When we had most of the issues back in the heyday, we had many security personnel over the building, but, gradually we started to lose our numbers and we needed more officers. So, with the lack of cameras and security, our school had two high profile sexual assault incidences. I noticed Dr. Strongman was furious because the district didn't take the steps to help solve the problem... until that April morning. So the parade of suits marched through the circus tent similar to a line of elephants in the library, and at the tail end of the line was Dr. Ringmaster, and gone was Dr. Strongman.

Chapter 3: A New Director Takes Control

I remember the line of suits with Dr. S. Ringmaster leading the way. I remember seeing Mr. A. Big-Top and Mr. D. Magician in the group, but I still can't remember who else was in that line. They sent the staff a memo through their email that addressed everyone... including parents. Here is what the memo, dated April 5, 2010, stated as Dr. Ringmaster read it to the faculty:

"Securing student safety and health is one of the highest priorities of Puzzle City Public Schools. I want to follow-up on the phone message we sent you yesterday (4-5-10) and offer more information about the incident that occurred recently at your school and the steps we will take to ensure a safe experience for Jane Austen High School students and staff."

"PCPS learned earlier this week that a student was allegedly the victim of a sexual assault at JAHS. An extensive internal investigation began immediately after we got notified of the incident. PCPS is cooperating with the Puzzle City Police Department as the official investigation continues. I immediately made personnel changes, and additional changes might be forthcoming pending the outcome of our investigation. Starting April 6th, Mr. Magician, Senior Director of School Leadership, took charge of the building during the school day pending any additional decisions regarding leadership and personnel at JAHS."

46

"It is crucial that you realize we take this incident seriously. As parents/guardians, you entrust your children to our care. It is our responsibility to ensure that your children are safe. I commit to taking the following steps to further protect students: (1) Continue to conduct extensive weekly safety reviews at the school. (2) Install alarms on doors in specific areas of the building. (3) Secure staff work area closed classrooms and restricting access to under-used building areas. (4) Reinforce adult supervision of students during lunch, recess and passing periods." [Except there isn't any "recess," in high school].

"It is imperative that every student and staff member is safe while at school to foster a productive learning environment. Please see that my team and I at PCPS are doing everything possible to make that happen."

Dr. Ringmaster had made the changes official; Dr. Strongman was out as principal and replaced with Mr. Magician. They put a few of my colleagues on administrative leave because the sexual assault on an autistic girl (which truly saddened me to hear) that happened around these teachers' classrooms was under investigation. The irony was when this event happened, I was not in school that day. After Dr. Ringmaster had read the memo, he stayed to thank every staff member for their 'hard work'. I will say that I considered not even acknowledging my superintendent, but then I changed my mind. I needed to see what his reaction would be to my shaking his hand since we last met in January.

Just like the cool, composed figurehead he tried to be, Dr. Ringmaster firmly shook my hand and thanked me for maintaining the course through all the troubles our school had faced. Did Dr. Ringmaster honestly have any idea who I was and what he had ordered to do to me? In my imagination, I'd really wanted to assume he saw actually who I was and had then wished he had tried to dodge me knowing what he did... but, that didn't happen. Dr. Ringmaster just shook the weirdo's hand, thanked me for my service and dawdled about his business as if he has no clue who he just met.

Any redemption or a longing miracle with Dr. Strongman and my position with the district just got obliterated. The detailed story of the assault cases and the lack of security is a tale that is best told by Dr. Strongman. I will say that in an exclusive article from the Puzzle City Times on June 6, 2010, Dr. Strongman did just that! Here are a few details from that interview: Dr. Strongman's frustrations with the school district started relatively early when he first came on board. He clearly saw several security issues with the school. Not enough security personnel, lack of security cameras, broken or dysfunctional door locks showed to be considerably glaring problems.

Sure enough, those issues played into the sexual assaults on two female students in the J. Austen school. One female previously had a history of sexual assault at home while the other was an autistic girl! To say that Dr. Strongman was furious with the head administrator for downtown Puzzle City didn't say it enough. Dr. Ringmaster had promised Dr. Strongman he actually could help in securing Jane Austen High School down, but that wasn't to be a promise he'd keep. Based on my own observations, I had to agree with Dr. Strongman. There were no new security people or cameras. I wasn't sure about the locks on the doors. The main thing Dr. Strongman wanted was a clean, safe environment where students may learn without the apparent distractions they had experienced two years ago.

PEEKING UNDER THE TENT: Dr. E. Strongman

I'm taking a moment to be a curious onlooker in the mind of the different people in this book. I can only imagine what each person is considering or thinking, but I will try my best from the perspective of a weirdo with Asperger's Syndrome. I always understood that Dr. Strongman implied to be a journeyman. I say this because he had been in administration across the United States. I found him to be a unique leader. I'd have to call him the best 'teaching' principal I had the chance to work within any school setting. If you're not sure what I mean, the best way I can describe him is that he would watch your class, and offer excellent suggestions to help enhance you as a teacher. Dr. Strongman was a student of the mechanics of a well-run class. He might legitimately look outside the box at things most regular administrators miss. I'm not referring to content; it's more of a class arrangement or teacher placement within the room. I understood he wanted to have the best faculty to support any student that came into his building. I see that working for the district tested his patience and vision he wanted for everyone.

With the change in leadership established, and the bandwagon ready, this statement was the first thing our new principal told the students:

April 7, 2010

"To the students of J. Austen High School,

This past week was very difficult for everyone on campus. We understand that fulfilling your obligations as students are difficult if you don't recognize what is happening. We further see that you care for the people directly affected. I want to help clarify the situation and ease your concerns."

"They had placed several JAHS staff members on administrative leave while a full investigation took place. Because of laws on the confidentiality of a person's employment records, I can share nothing more with you. This is the law, and they design it to

protect employee rights. Each employee placed on leave will help with the investigation and explain what happened last week. I have made no final decisions on any staff member.

By identifying where things stand, my goal is to move forward as a unified team of students and staff. Beginning today, we must start doing what we require in making JAHS the school that it should be, a place where everyone feels safe and secure and can get an excellent education. Together, we will make this a great year for our school. On behalf of the entire PCPS administration, the JAHS staff, and me: thank you for helping us achieve this mission."

** Mr. D. Magician {PCPS Senior Director of School Leadership}*

As I mentioned in the beginning, this story is concerning awareness and forgiveness, and for Mr. Magician, it would take some time for him to gain my forgiveness moving forward, and you will see why. As I stated earlier, my first impression of him was of a smug man, and I'd wanted to consider I was perhaps way off in my evaluation, but Mr. Magician made the reconsideration difficult. I'll let you be the ultimate judge on his first comments to the students, but I believe you can literally read the ego just oozing through the text. Little did I perceive that his narcissistic self will hit me very hard right in the face just two days after Mr. Magician's letter.

On the morning of April 9, 2010, when I was preparing my lessons for that day, I never might have imagined how the administration prepared for the attack. The first wave started in my 3rd-hour class. The vice-principal Ms. Puppet appeared openly in my room. Now, granted, I'd realized an observation would be coming, but I just didn't know when. As she made her observation, I continued with my business, teaching the class and in my mind, I honestly considered the class to be a well-behaved group of students. Then the second wave rolled in during the very next hour, 4th hour. This observation surprised me slightly more because the person was my Social Studies Coordinator, Ms. A. Juggler! I have to admit, it was ludicrous because she came in as if she wasn't observing but I could easily tell otherwise. She had told me she just wanted to see how things were going and to tell me that Mr. Popcorn may not return to 'support' in reviewing the students in government because they didn't pay attention. Then she left with her small notebook.

I guess I need to explain the story of Mr. Popcorn and his guest appearance in my government class. The idea was to have a fairly old colleague of mine who retired, come back to my class and give the students extra help. Mr. Popcorn had been the government teacher before I took the reins. I remember having a discussion with the Social Studies Coordinator, Ms. Juggler and Mr. Popcorn with this idea of him returning toward the start of the school year. Mr. Popcorn said he wanted to model what he did to have a successful class. I told them I didn't mind him coming in; however, I tried to warn him that these students are not the best bunch in the world.

I remember the classes he had, and this was not it! I taught the classes the whole time until on April 2nd, out of nowhere, Mr. Popcorn showed up and spoke in both of my government classes with a booklet in hand. The ironic part of Mr. Popcorn's visit was that he truly didn't 'model' any classroom instruction. I think our original discussion on what he had done for my class either changed because of my circumstances or he forgot...I'm genuinely not sure. I still hold the greatest respect for Mr. Popcorn. I mean, when I started in the district back in 1996 at the Middle School, he was there with me as part of the staff since day one. He and I always had a wonderful working relationship.

The April 12th observation train finally ended with the 3rd wave, 7th hour, with a visit from our new 'leader,' Mr. D. Magician. I will describe what happened the way I did to my NEA on the April 10th email. "Mr. Magician comes in, unannounced, and asks if the students in my room were completely mine. I tell him truthfully that they are not. He leaves and returns with our two [Resource Officers] RSO

Officers. (These are actual Puzzle City Michigan Police Officers. The school district has its own security officers, but Mr. Magician chooses our Puzzle City, Michigan's finest instead.) Mr. Magician takes my roster and goes around to every student and weeds out the ones out of place in the class. He tells me to see him after school. At the end of school, I met with him in Dr. Strongman's old office. He tells me I need to only have my students and no one else. I told him how originally the plan was to just write the names of students and turn the list into Mr. R. Parade (the other vice-principal). Mr. Magician either didn't understand or didn't care, he simply said I did not comply. He didn't want to see that again and that he would write a letter out explaining the incident and what my direct responsibility was.

The best way I might describe our little 'meeting', or more of what appears to be a scolding from a parent is it seemed as if I was a young child who disobeyed his father. I realized, though, the persons I sympathized with were our two PC police officers. I appreciated both gentlemen rather well. I had them come into my room to talk to my students concerning the Bill of Rights. They loved it! The kids asked questions about what they did and the police got the chance to explain why it was important to learn your rights. I realized this was a wonderful ambassadorship to bring goodwill to the students and the police force... but no, this was how Mr. Magician saw our RSO officers — as the cleanup crew.

In my fourteen years at Puzzle City, Michigan, literally my entire teaching career which spanned since 1991, I have never received an open reprimand from any administrator. Until April 13th. In realizing the actual purpose of this letter, this reprimand would be the spearhead to have me fired from the district. Here is the letter in its entirety:

J. Austen High School

Date: April 13, 2010

To: Xander A. Bell

From: Mr. D. Magician

Re: Letter of Reprimand

On Monday, April 12, 2010, I conducted an informal classroom observation in your classroom. While sitting in your classroom, you admitted that some students stroll in to be in your room. The only reason that you admitted was because [sic] I asked why the students were not working. After checking your roster, I asked the twelve students not on the roster to step out into the hallway.

Your classroom is an unsafe student-learning environment. There was little or no learning to take place in your classroom because there are no rules, consequences, rewards, or procedures. Furthermore, I see that your failure to enforce school rules and norms and failure to insist that students report to their assigned classrooms jeopardizes the safety of this entire building. Therefore, you are receiving this letter of reprimand to make clear that my expectations is [sic] for you not allowing students to skip their assigned class to hide in your classroom.

Improvement Suggestions:

1.Develop a classroom management plan to handle minor students' behaviors.
2.Submit a copy of your classroom management plan to me so that I can approve it.
3.Once approved, post your classroom management plan (e.g. rules, consequences, rewards).
4.Do not allow any students not assigned to your classroom to skip classes in your room.
5.Report major problems to the principal.

In closing, I want you to have a successful teaching experience, but you must improve your teaching performance. It is up to you to improve. If you have questions concerning this memorandum, you may put them in writing no later than Friday, April 16, 2010, or you can see Ms. Monday [I guess that was a secretary but, I don't remember anyone by that name] in the main office to schedule a meeting to discuss this letter of reprimand.

Sincerely,

Mr. D. Magician, Ed. S.

Acting Principal

Xander Bell [Signature] Date: 4-13-10

Cc: (The Vice-Principal)

Personnel File

And that was that. You can then guess why I absolutely didn't give a crap about the damn letter — because he informed me he would fire no matter what... so this letter was just a bullying tactic on Mr. Magician's part to rattle my nerves. The letter was just one of those things you don't expect when you've constantly been hammered down by observations, meetings, PGP and NODS. I have to admit the letter is kind of funny now that I've revisited it: 1. The way he described the incident isn't entirely how it happened (as I detailed before the letter), 2. In his 4th 'suggestion' I love how he determined the skipping kids was completely my fault, you see; as if I *really* wanted the students in my room. and 3. In his 5th 'suggestion' I believe he jumbled the sentences. I consider the comment needed to read "Report: The major problem IS the principal."

I found the email where Dr. Strongman and I had a procedure where I teach the class, write the names and turn them into the vice-principal, Mr. Parade. I emailed Mr. Magician as evidence to prove him wrong, but I got no reply... shocked? I'm just surprised he hadn't questioned my manhood! Now looking back, I did not notice how he could've gotten a letter placed in my personnel file. I really need to look at my personnel file to see what else is in there. In my journal, I even wrote a prayer for Mr. Magician saying, "Lord, he needs your help." I meant what I said. I saw he was way out of compliance further than any other person I had dealt with, and it compelled me to pray for him.

On April 15th, during my Sixth Hour class, my Social Studies coordinator, Ms. Juggler had again returned unannounced. The coordinator made her way to the back of the room and made notes on the pad while the class continued. Remember, the last time the coordinator made an appearance, she just came in to tell me that Mr. Popcorn wasn't going to be returning with her second trip in as many days threw me slightly. The coordinator stayed with me after Sixth Hour moving into the last hour of the day as she continued to take notes. I was getting somewhat unnerved by this time, so I decided I'd give her some information and see if I might pry any reason she's in my room. I told her that several of these government students cannot take the test End Of Course [EOC] test for government because they were not only doing completely failing in class but would underperform on the mock EOC test.

Nothing... that's the response I got... nothing. Ms. Juggler didn't ask me if I needed any resources or help this time, she just stayed only for the first part of the Seventh Hour, left and didn't tell me why she was in my class. Remember, this was the person I had worked with for a few years before she moved to the main office. I just couldn't believe it. I just wondered if they gave the coordinator the ultimatum of 'do as I say or you can join Mr. Bell's fate.' If we switched roles, I believe that may be a hard decision. I mean, literally, Ms. Juggler had many more important things to do than to just get dragged in and forced to observe one damn Social Studies teacher when she handles every other Social Studies teacher in the whole district! An odd footnote to that day, the vice-principal Ms. Puppet kept looking into my room, but she never entered. I wasn't sure what that was about.

Well, at least the vice-principal Ms. Puppet made an actual appearance four days later on April 19th. The vice-principal selected my second hour Government class unannounced, and she stayed awhile. The vice-principal looked at the material on my board and my lesson plans. I realized the students had done an excellent job; they took part in the exercise. Again, I'm sure there was something where they'd say I screwed up, just to get any dirt they could; however, it's worth noting, that this visit would be my vice-principal Ms. Puppet's last. I guess deep down, I perceived she didn't want to be the headhunter.

I believe my vice-principal was witnessing a level of unprofessionalism she had never seen before or, in this case, a serious disregard for 'proper' administration duties. I guess you might say I felt awful for her. In essence, Ms. Puppet scheduled visits to my class on April 21st, April 23rd, and she told me she would visit my Third Hour class on May 3rd but, it turned out to be a no-show. May 5th was the next visit she skipped, and for May 6th, she told me she might visit my First Hour class, but didn't show either. Finally, she scheduled a visit with me on May 13th but elected not to come then either.

Ms. Juggler paid another, unannounced visit to my humble classroom on April 18th. Ms. Juggler entered at the very end of Third Hour and stayed through most of my Fourth Hour. She sat down and started taking notes again. Because of the coordinator's job, I finally got compelled to ask her concerning these 'sudden' observations she was having to do. I wished my coordinator might have said something regarding the truth, and that she had her orders. Instead, this was the answer I received, "I have to do these observations at the end of the year. I have you and others from Social Studies, Math, Science, etc. It's just crazy with everything else." I honestly believe the only true statement was "It's just crazy with everything else." I realized one sentence from the coordinator rang volumes; sadly, I was too disappointed to grasp the real meaning. Once, I told her 'okay' and continued with my business. After Ms. Juggler left, I asked the three of my fellow Social Studies Teachers if Ms. Juggler had been in their rooms and all of them said she hadn't been to their rooms. In fact, they didn't realize she was in the building!

I even went further and asked one middle school science teacher and one high school math teacher if the coordinator had observed their class, and they told me "no". I want to believe the coordinator was telling the truth, but so far, after two separate visits, that didn't look to be the case. In my email to my NEA rep., I informed her about this last visit and how I still hadn't heard from Mr. Magician regarding my rebuttal to his letter. In reality, the district should destroy the letter since Mr. Magician didn't even discuss my counter-argument that I was correct with the method Dr. Strongman and I had agreed to with the plan.

The rep Ms. Warrior told me to file an EEOC (Equal Employment Opportunity Commission) complaint that night on being observed/tested without notice and by a party not identified as an observer on the district's NOD. She pointed out that this violated my agreed-upon accommodations with the district. The rep stepped up the pressure on the district. Honestly, by this point, every time my door opened, I jumped in fear. The constant visits were taking a toll on me. I was not giving up, but I was getting close. The pressure was ramping up and I realized that if I could just hold on for a while, I'd make it through the unprofessional treatment I was receiving.

PEEKING UNDER THE TENT: Mr. D. Magician

My first impression of his demeanor was — I considered he was in the wrong line of work. Mr. Magician might make an incredible politician, and I'm serious. He has that combination of wit, looks, arrogance and ruthlessness one needs to be a councilman or even mayor. (Not bad for a former librarian.) At one point, he had plagiarized his own thesis for his doctorate. The deception was discovered and he later withdrew his title in shame until he found a way to make it up. I have to admit that if the roles were reversed, I honestly don't see how I'd handle the job they put in him by Dr. Ringmaster. I understand following the orders can be difficult, especially if it meant either get rid of me or get fired. There is a wide gap between leadership and bullying. With the harsh attacks and threats, this leads me to believe he genuinely enjoyed tormenting me hoping he'd witness me getting trampled under the tremendous pressure. One thing I learned for sure with

Mr. Magician is that he's in the position of leadership, not from talent or skill, but in knowing the right people to place him there… just like a politician.

Before the anticlimactic meeting with Dr. M. Clown on April 23rd, Mr. Magician was up to his—what was rapidly getting old—shenanigans. On April 22nd, during my Second Hour class, I allowed a female student to go get a drink of water. From my memory, she was a very responsible kid, and I perceived it normally shouldn't be an issue… however, when she returned, she got escorted by Mr. Magician. He questioned me about a student getting a drink without a pass. I told him yes, I had allowed it. (Can you tell I didn't give a crap regarding him and his use of bullying tactic again.) He reminded me that every student needs a pass before leaving the room. So I said okay I'll remember that next time. Problem solved… right?

A little later, I sent another student out with a pass to the restroom and when he returned, he told me that Mr. Magician had questioned him on why he had to use the restroom right now. He suggested that the student needed to use the bathroom during passing time. Then a few moments later, I noticed a few students without passes walking around the hallway… must be nice. I remember shaking my head and reminding myself that I was a walking target. Now, on to the meeting!

Dr. Clown wanted to meet with my rep and me, but we got to add one person and she was my autism advocate. The advocate worked with the state of Michigan, but this was a personal favor, and I certainly appreciated her company and insight. I don't have a bunch of information concerning this meeting because it was just a waste of time. The only reasonable thing we accomplished was giving Dr. Clown a letter my psychologist had written that proved I did unquestionably have the disability, and my doctor even told her what my accommodations should be for a person in my condition. If I remember correctly, I believe she had wanted proof that I genuinely had the disorder and my advocate accompanied me to help offer any supplementary explanation or clarification Dr. Clown might have needed with the letter.

Sadly, the only real thing Dr. Clown wanted to identify as if I was finally giving up and quitting the district. This was that literal moment of truth. I remember Gaby and I talking about this issue at great length. We discussed how she had wished she fought against the school district in her case; however; she ended up settling. Sometimes in my past, I wished I had fought for my earlier jobs instead of just giving up and resigning. This time was different. This time enough was enough! What sounded like a simple question had transformed into an ultimate line in the sand moment. Do I give up as I've done in the past, or do I stand and fight for me and everyone else with

Autism Spectrum Disorder? Deep down, I realized what might happen, and I was afraid. If I didn't stand up, what happens to those who end up in the same plight? We decided.

My rep Ms. Warrior could easily answer the question based on my expression, but she still asked, "**What do I tell Dr. Clown?**"

I remember looking at Ms. Warrior and telling her: "**Please inform Dr. Clown, I'll be staying on until the end of the school year.**" Thus, I sealed my fate.

Chapter 4: Removing The Curtain

I had previously experienced a great amount of pressure already. Why give up now? The school year was ending in a month and there was no reason to give up now. I remember leaving the office and waiting out in the guest section for my NEA rep. I was just talking with my advocate when the rep Ms. A. Warrior finally came out with a noticeably-disturbed look on her face. I wanted to ask what happened, but knowing my rep, I figured she'd tell me later why she was so irritated. I expected the meeting was just a time-eater, but I learned later that was not the reason. They'd given descriptive orders on my future with the school district. I wasn't there, but my rep said, "When I spoke with Dr. M. Clown, she told me what the mandated top-secret orders were."

The only thing I knew at that moment was my rep was having a difficult time telling me what that order was. But I had to know. I had to learn what may finally get to the core of this whole 'witch hunt'. I had to know why this school year had turned ugly incredibly fast for me.

My rep finally relented because she recognized that I had to have the truth, "Dr. Clown stated this was the directive: 'They told me to **get rid of the weirdo**.' The final orders were very explicit, and they commanded the district to do their best to follow them."

On April 26th, an odd thing happened that completely threw both Dr. Clown and Mr. Magician. As a teacher, we have needs; there are a few specific things we need rather more immediate than others. They can be basic things like... going to the restroom. You can guess that's not actually a big issue, but when you're a teacher with a classroom of students and law requires you never to leave them alone, that can complicate things.

On this day, during my Third Hour class, I had to use the restroom. The procedure was to call the security phone and if they don't answer, then call the office and let them know of your dilemma. I tried to phone the security desk, but the phone was busy, so I continued to Plan B and called the office. Their best advice for me was to "try to find somcone" helpful. The third hour ended, Fourth Hour begins, no one during the passing period to help, the new hour started, and I needed to go... badly. I finally got a hold of security only to find out they can't be by themselves in the classroom. Just great. I wondered why I called them in the first place!

Toward the end of the Fourth Hour Mr. Magician and, of all people, Dr. Clown came by my room! I'M SAVED — by the two people who were the biggest problems for my job. My knight in shining armor, Mr. Magician, was ready to pounce on me concerning a female student if she was a member of my class. By this point, I literally didn't care. I had to badly use the restroom, and it may have Dr. Ringmaster and his entire circus and I couldn't care less; I had to use it now! So I boldly cut off Mr. Magician and explained I had been waiting for someone to take my class so I could use the facilities. To my actual surprise, Mr. Magician said he'd watch the class. (I imagine he presumably expected this might be a good opportunity to question the students regarding me, but I truly didn't want to know and I didn't care.) I told him before I left that all the students in my class were actually mine, knowing his sarcastic nature. During the time I finally used the restroom, the bell rang for the Fifth Hour.

When I returned to my classroom, Mr. Magician had pulled a disappearing act and there, standing alone, was Dr. Clown. I asked her what was going on. Dr. Clown chuckled at the irony of my question, but she told me she wasn't even here for me, it was for enrollment. I judged her statement concerning being here for enrollment was partially true, but what stumped me was why she was on the 3rd floor?

I can only speculate that they might have met with the vice-principal because I received a late meeting date for Wednesday, April 28th. This was not a coincidence. Strangely, during my plan time (Fifth Hour), I discovered a student had put superglue on my doorknob as a joke. I saw the glue before I put my hand on the handle thankfully, so I informed Mr. Magician and security about the prank.

Security complained to me regarding the lack of cameras in my location to see who might have done this. Mr. Magician had no comment. I guess I saw this moment as an oxymoron because here I've been, following Mr. Magician and his instructions, but when stupid stuff like the super glue happens, this just further shows how I was getting pushed out the door on things that were out of my control. It looked like I had to miraculously classroom-manage the entire building!

Here's the doorknob which had the Super Glue on it.

The meeting with the vice-principal happened on Thursday, April 29th. This get-together revolved around my Notice of Deficiency Review. The two areas they were aiming at were *"Standard 1, Teacher ensures instruction leads to student engagement, problem-solving and higher-level reasoning skills,"* and Standard 3, *"Teacher implements effective classroom management to maximize student learning."* You realize the irony here was that the whole school was in complete chaos so, for any teacher, classroom management is a much greater challenge when there are plenty of distractions all over the school. (Oh yes, don't forget, April is Autism Awareness Month.) Anyway... The vice-principal Ms. Puppet broke down the observations and the findings by date and hour, but what she didn't add was each evaluator, but I'll be happy to fill in the gaps:

The first reported evaluation was dated April 8th, during my Fourth Hour period. (Although the date was April 8th, it was really the third hour, and the evaluator was the vice-principal Ms. Puppet).

- *20 students in class 5 with heads down*
- *1 student in class who did not belong there (skipping)*
- *Teacher writing notes on board but not instructing students to take notes so only one student did*
- *3 cell phones out*

The second reported evaluation was on April 8th during my Fifth Hour period (Yep, same day but, the wrong hour again, since my plan was the Fifth Hour, this happened during the Fourth Hour and the evaluator was the Social Studies coordinator Ms. Juggler).

• Observed the same student from the 4th (3rd) period who did not belong there in class again
• Observed a friend of the above student in the classroom during this period.
• Later that day checked schedules and neither of them belonged in the class.

The third reported evaluation was April 8th during my Seventh Hour period (Part 1) [Yep still the same day and finally the information is correct and the evaluator was Mr. Magician].

• 12 students not on the roster were sitting in the classroom (skipping)
• Lack of procedures, norms, and consequences

The fourth reported evaluation was April 9th during my Sixth Hour period [This took place in Sixth and Seventh Hour but, this got split up into two separate observations and the evaluator was Social Studies coordinator].

• History Channel concerning the Cuban missile crisis; not following the 40-day plan given by the district
• One student in the classroom computer playing
• Group of students sitting in a circle discussing the taste of green tea, pineapple or salsa (That's not a joke; it actually happened)
• Boy and a girl sitting in the back, holding hands and talking
• Rest of class on cell phones, talking or sleeping

• One student watching the movie
• Seventh Hour (Part 2)
• Several students came in late, the teacher asked but no passes and they gave a reason
• Bell rang at 1:41 but the class did not start until 1:53
• Class worked for five minutes and then talked and played the remaining time

The fifth reported evaluation was April 14th during my second hour period [All correct and the evaluator was the vice-principal].

• 12 students in the class
• 2 sitting in the back, talking
• 3 students with cell phones out and 1 with headphones in
• 4 students sitting together turned towards each other talking

• At 9:07 the lesson gets finished because all but one are engaged in private off-task conversations, and no work is being done.
• For the entire class period, I may find only three students working.

This was how the NOD was summarized by Ms. Puppet the vice-principal:

"The standards noted above that needed addressing and corrected are still deficient. Mr. Bell has not implemented a satisfactory classroom management plan to manage and improve student behaviors, nor has he developed explicit procedures and routines to maximize student learning. Mr. Bell again needs to make sure that instruction leads to student engagement, problem-solving and higher-level study skills, and he has not met this either. The number of students who still come into his classroom and put their heads down, engage in off-task behavior and use their electronic devices has not improved."

I didn't sign off on this stupidity until May 7th though. With a twist of irony on May 3rd, they offered me a teaching contract for the next year! I wasn't really surprised since I wasn't fired or quit, I was still an employee of the district so HR had to send a new contract. I want to share an entry in my personal journal that I wrote for the week of May 2nd through 7th, because not only do I explain the signing off, but I also express my feelings as the school year was coming to a close. This is what I wrote:

"Becoming even closer! (To the end of the year) This was the Seniors' last week at Jane Austen High School, so I realize they're excited. Lord be with every one of them as they transition from high school to whatever. Didn't hear much from NEA rep, Ms. Warrior, this week. I never received a visit as vice-principal promised, so I signed off on the summary of earlier evaluations… and that was it. I didn't understand what's going on with these evaluations. All I have is that You (Lord) see everything and You see what's happening. I just give it all to you, Lord. Classes progressed okay this week, but I can't wait until it's over and done. I guess I'm tired of all the nonsense. JAHS had been going through some renovations, but it didn't make a difference in the problems the school was having. Ironically, this week was teacher apprehension… not enjoying it. Lord, give me the strength to just make it through the week." Little did I realize that my school year concludes in 11 days.

On May 14th, the final unscheduled observation I received came from the instructional coach, who came in unannounced (surprised?). She stood at one end of the room taking notes about the students and not asking me any questions. As the instructional coach was leaving, I told her I hadn't seen the results of the End Of Course test, so she informed me they had extended the date. I assumed I was through with the evaluation, so I went on with my last hour until... HE returned. Yes, roughly ten minutes later, Mr. Magician barges in the room, unannounced, walks over to one of my students and asks her a question. He takes a quick look and leaves without question, which left me puzzled, considering he always had to have some sort of ignorant comment before he would make a grand exit. I later asked the student what he wanted. She told me he wanted to know what she was doing. The student said 'working on a worksheet' and all I could do was laugh. What a terrific comment she made. And... I didn't get any feedback, but all the teachers got an email later that evening:

{When you read this, I want you to note the way he writes this letter. I will bolden some keywords.}

Subject: Kudos and Expectations

From: Mr. D. Magician

Sent: Friday, May 14, 2010 6:35 PM

Dear Colleagues,

Please permit me this opportunity to express my personal appreciation for the efforts you have made over the past five weeks since my arrival. We have continued to put emphasis on safety, and we have successfully concluded our MAP and EOC testing. I particularly wish to thank [instructional coach] for her leadership, hard work and dedication in planning, facilitating and wrapping up this year's testing successfully.

Teachers, I thank you for your role in facilitating the state tests. Under your direction, many of our students have represented J. Austen High School well, and I am positive that this will show up on state exam results. For this, I say thank you for a job well done.

*As we close this academic year, let me **remind everyone that there aren't any instructional days that one can label as being unimportant or expendable**. The last day of school is as important as the first. The waning days of the semester can have an enormous impact on a student's impression of a course and teacher. The end of the year cannot dissipate the efforts and achievements of an entire school term. In the **final days, we must sway from idleness or frivolity** (means lack of seriousness). What I have carefully constructed and developed can collapse if we do not invest in the same effort that ran into our first days in these last days.*

*We can meet the challenges of late May. The proof was very clear to the administration as we walked around the building. We found meaningful instruction going on in most classrooms. I commend you, my teachers, who have been teaching bell to bell. Keep up the fine work. **Let me be explicit**, that my expectation for* *these final seven days of school, is that each and every person prepare lessons that keep the students engaged from the first bell to the dismissal bell. With commitment and resolve, we can continue to make the end of school as exciting as the beginning.*

Last, we will have a staff meeting after school on Monday, May 24, 2010, at 3:01 p.m. At the faculty meeting, we will discuss end-of-year closeout procedures and expectations. We will further discuss the procedures for how we will use the new gates in the stairwells, and the roles and responsibilities for teachers, security, and maintenance relating to the gates. You will receive information on our end-of-year faculty luncheon.

Thank you,

Mr. Magician

*Mr. D. Magician, Ed.S./Sr. Director, School Leadership & **Acting Principal at the "New" J. Austen High School***

Address of School/School Number

First... yes, I took a picture of the gated stairwell mentioned in Mr. Magician's email. And second, I don't understand why they build a gate, windows, and paneling on every set of upper stairs. (See Photo.)

As you might tell, this email looks more like they wrote it for children more than for professional educators. I found it considerably demeaning. Remember, we were talking seven more days of school...7... that's all. The school year was long, I mean long and tiring. No teacher needed to hear the intellectual babbling of a principal who wasn't a part of all the chaos until the end and honestly, no teacher cared; they just might not wait until summer. I believe you now have a good idea of what kind of (I use this loosely) leader Mr. Magician was. I'll never forget the one thing that stood out the most from that email was the tagline at the end, the "New J. Austen High School." That statement he had no business saying because he was coming at the end of the year, nothing really changed with the craziness of the building and had Dr. Strongman had all the rapid improvements to secure the building like he asked, he presumably may still have been principal.

They scheduled a meeting for Monday, May 17th, but my NEA rep was not in town and could not be available until Wednesday, May 19th at 11:45. This happened during my lunchtime, but I was fine because my plan time was the next hour. I didn't understand what this meeting would be regarding. The end of school was coming, and I had heard nothing from the administration, NEA or human resources. I expected the meeting might have involved another NOD or PGP review, which might not have been surprised, but I wasn't sure so I continued to the main office and met with my NEA rep. Ms. Warrior. I only had a second to ask her how she was before the instructional coach came into the office and said she was asked to escort me to the meeting room as if I was a guest of honor. My entry into the conference room felt like going full circle. This was the room where everything started, and now this is where my journey came to the end.

As my rep and I walked through the threshold one last time, we were greeted by a considerably over-jubilant Mr. Magician seated at the far end of the rectangular conference table like some CEO, and seated to his right was the vice-principal Ms. Puppet. I vaguely remember two folders in front of Mr. Magician, but the one thing that surprised me was the vice-principal. As I moved toward Mr. Magician, I noticed a visibly upset vice-principal Ms. Puppet, and even my rep had observed she might have been crying. I will admit this it confounded me, but when I saw her reaction, it made sense. She perceived this whole witch hunt was wrong. I believe she did not agree with the spiteful orders given to her.

Obviously, this didn't matter to Mr. Magician who was all smiles as he officially announced to me they have put me on administrative leave, and I had 20 minutes to get all my things out of the building. He then added more detail, although my rep could have told me the same information. He informed me I was being barred from any Puzzle City Public School property; I could not be in contact with any PCPS employee (which wasn't true), and that formal charges for my termination will take place. With that, he shot up, shook my hand with a huge grin on his face, and wished me all the best. Mr. Magician suggested that he can have one of his security guards escort me outside the building, but my completely anointed NEA rep would have none of that, and she told Mr. Magician that she will make sure we vacate the building.

Once we left, my rep Ms. Warrior, and I made our way back to my classroom. I promptly started taking all the things that were mine. Fortunately, I had gradually started taking things out of my room throughout the last part of the school year, knowing full well I would not be returning. Ms. Warrior took some pictures of the room before we left. As she was taking the pictures, I had some mixed reaction with this moment. It relieved me that the bullying and harassing were over, but I just wished I had stayed until the end. The cleanout didn't totally take me 20 minutes, but it was close. With all the stuff in tow, I looked to see if security was going to drag me out. I took one last look around the room full of great memories, and I tried to keep a good frame of mind remembering my classes. Ms. Warrior asked if I was ready.

I hesitated for a moment, but I relented, she and I departed the J. Austen High School for the last time. No 'thank you' celebrations for the 14 years of service. No 'best of luck' in my future endeavors. Just get out of the building. After we left, the rep and I talked out in the parking lot. She took a hard look at me to see how I was handling the prompt ejection from the building and asked if I was all right. I was still surprised that this happened, but I guess I realized deep down that this was inevitable. Ms. Warrior told me that the NEA legal team would presumably get in touch with me in the dealings once they file the charges to the school board. The curtain closed and the legal battle was on the horizon.

CIRCUS RING #2

(CENTER RING)

Chapter 5: A New Act Takes The Stage

My NEA Attorney — I'll call her Shelly for ID purposes — first got a hold of me on May 19, 2010, via email; the same day as my parting celebration from the district. She told me she would represent me pending my termination charges. The first thing my rep Ms. Warrior and I had to do was to send every piece of information to Shelly so she could pour through all the evidence we had collected. I will say that was difficult, time-consuming, and frustrating because I had to pull up lots of emails and old memos. I will have to admit that in this second part of this story, there might be some legal jargon and broken-down observations of documents, especially on the PGP's and the NOD.

To give a good example of what I'm referring to, Shelly made an observation about a date April 13th, and this was what she asked:

"So is the April 13th letter what they believe to be the notice of deficiencies? And they intended the timeline for action steps to be the remediation plan? Not only did they not follow their own plan, but if they intend the April 13th reprimand letter to be the warning, I don't believe it complies with the statute. Very interesting."

Shelly

As you might have guessed, Shelly was referring to the letter of reprimand I received from Mr. Magician, and I found this interesting that she was questioning whether this letter had anything to do with my PGP or if it was an action step. Either way, she concluded that the letter was a misuse of power or out of compliance with my PGP. Since I already had a plan in place, Mr. Magician stepped out-of-bounds by adding to my set of guidelines and adding more "suggestions" as he called it. With her legal opinion, I believe the letter should be out of my file since this was an abuse of power.

Basically, we spent the rest of May and parts of June giving our NEA attorney all the information we had on my case. One decision that my wife and I both agreed on was that we absolutely didn't want to settle with the school district. Gaby had already been through that as I mentioned earlier, and I didn't go through all of that harsh mistreatment just to betray my wife's confidence. I was ready to fight the district all the way to the very end. With our NEA attorney doing her research, Gaby and I decided we needed to meet with an outside lawyer who had experience with school law but was not linked to either the district or the NEA. Our goal was to see if my discrimination case with the district might call for a lawsuit.

We were trying to be proactive instead of the charges being filed against my termination. The NEA had a list of recommended lawyers in town who might be good to speak with, so we contacted one firm. They said they would meet with us, so right away Gaby and I appeared confident in our chances of having our case picked up by a lawyer.

On Friday, June 18th, we traveled to downtown Puzzle City and met with two attorneys to explain what happened to me and the district. When Gaby and I got introduced to the first lawyer, the whole office atmosphere looked impressive, and we were also impressed by our first discussion with the lawyer. Enter the school expert lawyer, and suddenly my wife's pleasant mood took a dark turn. I have to admit that my wife kept her composure when she entered, although, when the first attorney introduced the second to us, my wife stated: *"you don't have to introduce us, we've already met."*

At once, we realized there might be a real problem. The reason the second lawyer comprehended school law so well was because she used to be one of the Puzzle City, Michigan school district's attorneys. And when Gaby was fighting with the school district with her case, she was the one representing the district against her! All four of us met, but when we left, Gaby believed we may reach a dead end with these attorneys. The lawyers wanted to see the information we had collected, so I emailed them all the material. Later they wanted more information, so I was trying to be encouraged, and then the day after, more information again came in. I began to feel confident this might work. However, just two days later, my luck changed. On June 20th, I received an email from the law firm:

"Xander. It was a pleasure to meet you. After reviewing the documents, we believe the case may be a difficult one and will, therefore, decline representation. We will send you a formal disengagement letter. We wish you the best in your future endeavors."

Honestly, that infuriated me. My anger wasn't so much about just being turned down, but going through all the work of getting all of that information and getting a four-sentence answer to 'why' they can't take me didn't sit well with me. So I emailed them a question. "Thank you for reviewing my case. The only question I have is what did I miss making this case more pliable?" My disordered is in rage mode. I'm amazed I spelled out the whole letter properly! I wanted a better comprehension of what the issue was. Thankfully, the lawyer was nice enough to write me back.

"I don't expect a single document or fact to make it more plausible. If you are interested in pursuing a claim, I recommend that you contact another attorney soon. I wish you the best." This not only didn't make me appear any better, but the statement still made even less sense to me! What was she talking about? "Make it more plausible"? Really? Then when I told

my wife, she was very good enough to remind me that the second attorney must have remembered her and said to the first lawyer they shouldn't take the case. I was still furious, but at least what my wife said made sense.

PEEKING UNDER THE TENT: Dr. M. Clown

The people in Human Resources are truly an interesting group, because most of the time, some members really do have your best interest at heart. Then you have the ones that just aren't helpful, and make you scratch your head in confusion. One thing I learned about the HR department for PCPS was their turnover rate. For Dr. Clown, she truly defied all logic. She never seemed confrontational with people but was quite clever to still get the job done. Ironically, I do the same thing. I realize she expected the whole case of getting me fired might be difficult because of all the people I'd mentioned. She was the only person who learned what the district did wrong and how hard it was to be fulfilling Dr. Ringmaster's directives. So really, her sneakiness should not have surprised me.

I wanted to take a minute to remind you why I wrote this book -— Awareness and Forgiveness. If they discriminate against you at work or some other environment, one thing you need to do is file your discrimination to the Human Rights office. The main office in Michigan is at our State Capital — Lansing, but if you live in a major metropolitan city, there might be a branch office, which I had in Puzzle City. I want to encourage anyone to have ADA accommodation on file with your school or workplace, because that will prove a base where if your rights get violated, then you will have the legal backing you need. I need to let everyone see that when you file the "Charge of Discrimination", then that information gets sent to the Fair Employment Practices Agency (FEPA) and the Equal Employment Opportunity Commission (EEOC). I exactly this, and I had signed off on my complaint on June 20th, 2010. I wish to share some excellent information that my NEA rep shared with me about the complaint: *"It's important that you name as many specific people from the district as possible (all admin by name, all observed colleagues)."*

"You should likewise get some response from the EEOC, at the very least a case number. Please call one of their offices and check the status of your complaint. The big question you need to be asking is: Where is it? Is it being reviewed? Have they sent a Right to Sue letter? What is the case number? Besides writing this down, ask for the agency to send you some email confirmations on this." Once the complaint is filed, then your case gets a number, you'll receive several documents to which a few of those will be legal material and a questionnaire, and make sure you fill that out completely.

Understand that I was trying to do everything in my power to prepare for a serious battle with the Puzzle City school district. I recognized that my NEA lawyer, Shelly, was not the person I needed to sue the district when if they fired me, and to be honest, the possibility scared me. I could see how this whole thing might shakedown. My mind kept imagining many scenarios on how this process may look and sound like. I was getting frustrated because it set nothing. Drafting out the 'Charges of Discrimination' was a good positive first step, but the law firm not taking the case pierced through my plan in a tailspin. I wasn't giving up, but finding firms that would take my particular problem wasn't going to be easy.

I guess the biggest frustration was that I was not physically disabled. You look at me and say, "I see nothing wrong with him?" The problem is that's not true. I recognize I have issues, and my Asperger's can really affect my ability to work the way other normal people expect me to do different tasks. So, trying to get ordinary people to understand my condition and how the school district rammed their own educational ethics down my throat and disregarding my accommodations, virtually to the point of almost-insanity, is difficult to explain. If I had a walker, a cane, a wheelchair or some other apparatus that could aid me in my physical movement, then my disability would be obvious, but when the ailment is unseen, so is my so-called discrimination... unseen.

July rolled in and I expected I'd hear something... from anyone. Strangely nothing really happened during the whole month, so I felt compelled to share this ironic but true story. If you notice the landscape of Puzzle City, it's divided. The two lakes, Silver and Huyck break up the metro city into several parts, but mainly there are people who live on the north side of the sister lakes and people of the south side. I lived in what we here call the 'Northland', and the entire Puzzle City School District is all south part of the lakes, near the Indiana State Border. So every morning I'd get up right before 6:00 a.m. and head south on I-69. Ultimately, I'd pass by the south of downtown and then get off at the Stokes Road exit. Turn left on Stokes road and continue east. There is a hospital further down which looks out of place, but the hospital is a top emergency hospital in the Puzzle City area. As I'd finally turn left onto Allen Road, the number of charter and private schools I literally pass by always astounded me. I might have to guess about five to six schools altogether. Understand that whenever I make that drive, I'm praying to God just about every single day.

Once you get past all the urbanization and make your way down Allen Road and those marvelous neighborhoods, you can't help but let your mind wander with different ideas. Fall is one of the most exquisite seasons I know, with the tree leaves turning bright oranges and reds lining the street. It just makes for a fascinating drive. I will never forget driving in my ivory 2003 Volkswagen Rabbit, and it looked like every time I go cruising down the road through those elegant tree line, it felt like soldiers honoring me to their neighborhood. I pleaded with God to save me from this job that made me suffer like a hamster running on his wheel. I wanted to walk away and move right into a whole new life that might be more profitable and with less stress.

The neighborhood didn't help since the area was gushing with old-established and expensive homes. The irony is shocking how there was an area school in PCPS being planted right in the middle of Richville. Understand that the school had some highly influential people that graduated, or at least attended, J. Austen High School: the Marx brothers who established G & H Marx real estate, F.F. Copp who was an award-winning director, and G. Wickham who is an actor starring in movies such as *Pride Zombie*, *Sense and Monsters*, and *The Bingley's Place*, just to name a few. Sadly, those days with those names were far gone. To pay the bills, this was the place I had to work; the job was never easy. The funny thing is that on that fateful day on May 2010, driving in and praying that same pleading message to God, the Lord finally answered, just not the way I dreamed it might happen.

PEEKING UNDER THE TENT: Dr. S. Ringmaster

I honestly am not sure where to start with him. They chose him to be the head of one of the largest school districts in the city. He's the one who is to lead his entire faculty and staff. Supposedly, this man earned a doctorate in education and has spent his career in the teaching field. So, one person told him something very true, the educational material we were giving our students was not being shared at home. Even worse, the parents would never ask their child if they had homework or what they learned. Nothing. I badly wanted the students to be prepared for the state test; however, the only thing the leader saw was how strange I was. Did he assume I was a first-year teacher? A substitute? A student-teacher? I honestly will never learn. All I realized was… he just saw me as a weirdo.

August became the moment of truth. On August 11th, I finally received what the whole NEA team was waiting for — my letter from the school district with the charges for termination. The funny part was that the letter was first sent without it being certified, then the next they sent it again, and this time it was a certified letter... surprised? Here is what the letter stated, omitting specific names and numbers:

School letterhead

August 11, 2010

Via Certified and Regular U.S. Postal Service (even though it needed to be certified)

94

Xander Bell [My Address]

Re: Xander Bell - Teacher termination hearing

Dear Mr. Bell:

On May 19, 2010, we placed you on paid administrative leave pending formal notification of charges to terminate your employment under the Michigan Teacher Tenure Act. PCPS will immediately move forward with terminating your indefinite contract as a permanent teacher by delivering to you a Notice of Charges and Right to Hearing letter and selecting a date for your teacher termination hearing. Specifically, the forthcoming charges will include, but will not be limited to, incompetence and/or inefficiency and/or insubordination which was not cured during the 30-day Notice of Deficiencies time period of 4/1/10 - 5/3/10.

As an alternative to PCPS seeking to end your contract as a tenured teacher, we are offering you the option to voluntarily resign from your position with PCPS by providing PCPS with a signed letter of resignation and signed General Release and Waiver by August 18, 2010, PCPS will pay Mr. Bell a lump sum of twenty-five hundred dollars. ($2,500.00) To schedule an appointment to execute the release by August 18, 2010, please contact me at (phone number) before August 15, 2010.

Sincerely,

PCPS Lawyer and Signature

Cc: (Chief Legal Counsel) and Dr. Clown, HR Director

Then the school district attached this information with the letter:

Xander A. Bell

1.Hire Date: August 21st, 1996
2.Displacement Date: May 19th, 2010
3.Retirement Eligible: No
4.Position: Teacher at JAHS
5.Reason for Displacement: Failure to meet the performance Standard 2 - Teacher ensures instruction leads to student engagement, problem-solving and higher-level reasoning skills and standard and Standard 3 - Teacher implements effective classroom management to maximize student learning.
6.Evidence:
7.PGP time frame 9/20/09 - 4/1/10: PGP not met

1.b. NOD review letter dated 4/28/10.
2.c. NOD time frame 4/2/10 - 5/13/10: NOD not met.
Witnesses:

Dr. M. Clown
Dr. E. Strongman
Ms. S. Puppet
Ms. A. Juggler

I guess I need a minute to explain teacher tenure. In the state of Michigan, we have Teacher Tenure from which you just read was acted by the Michigan government on July 17th, 2011. (I believe we revisited this in 2014) If a full-time teacher has signed a new contract with one school district for five straight years then on the sixth year that teacher earns tenure. Basically, a tenured teacher has more power at their disposal, meaning contracting for a new year can be extended and not required to be turned in as early as a non-tenured teacher. For their teacher evaluations, they're not as many as a non-tenured and they are very difficult to fire. For the state of Michigan, these are the 'legal' reasons a school can fire a teacher:

• If the teacher has a physical or mental condition that renders him or her unfit to instruct or associate with children.

• For immoral conduct.

• For incompetence, inefficiency or insubordination in the line of duty.

• For willful or persistent violation of Michigan's school laws or the local school district's published policies or regulations.

- For excessive or unreasonable absences.
- For conviction of a felony or a crime of moral turpitude.

If you remember from the letter, the school district decided that the best one for me was "For incompetence, inefficiency or insubordination in the line of duty." After reading my story so far, I can imagine that you might expect this reason is a bunch of crap and you might be right but, let's not forget Dr. Ringmaster's ultimate command... "***get rid of the weirdo***". One thing that never really came to me until now was the expense of any hearing for a teacher. After doing some homework for this book, I discovered something that was never mentioned to me when I was going through this harsh treatment — the cost of a hearing, with all the legal costs to pay for by the district, minus the teacher's legal fees, can be very, very high. There have been many articles written from newspaper websites to which they state the costs can easily go into six figures. Try to keep this in mind as I move forward with my crazy tale.

Literally, two events happened: the letter of charges against me and the first day of school. As an educator, the sense of school starting soon was still there, but not being there was strange. Since I had done this job for so long, you should just naturally prepare yourself for school. I will admit the impression was oddly comforting but weird with no school, no class, no place to be. Ultimately, I applied to two schools; I didn't apply anywhere else because I was already under contract! If the right school district had come along and offered me a position, I may have been happy to get out of the PCPS contract, but no one came a talkin' so I decided just to wait it out.

With the letter being released, I perceived things might move. My lawyer Shelly wanted to talk with me. Sadly, for her to meet with me, she had to travel across the entire state just to do this. The only thing that had me turning very sour on Shelly was that she believed my case had too many holes. Really? How the hell is this possible?!!! I had to wonder, did she assume I was being terminated because I was a horrible teacher? To me, Shelly made no sense. So Gaby and I finally agreed to meet with a lawyer that came recommended by my NEA rep.

On Sunday, August 15th, we met with the rep's lawyer friend, which I'll refer to as S & K, and the discussion suggested moving the same way it did last time. S & K asked for most of the emails, and then they did something different that I didn't expect — they tried to call Dr. E. Strongman, the instructional coach, and the vice-principal. What the lawyers were looking for might be witnesses to what happened to me during school hours. I understand what they were seeking; however; the problem was I believed no one was going to share what happened. Dr. Strongman never answered his phone and I don't blame him. He already had the newspaper article giving his testimony. Why should anyone get involved with any of the nonsense that happened with the district?

If I was him, I would have distanced myself as far as I can. Gaby and I were uncomfortable with this position because they wanted me to speak with another colleague who experienced the same condition along with their principals. Ultimately, Gaby and I decided the route S & K were taking would not work and basically, both parties decided this was not for the best. Gaby and I guessed we'd try one more time with another lawyer, so we contacted who I'll call BR. BR wanted all the information so I sent it to him but, ironically, we found out that we couldn't sue the school district while the state was still investigating the matter. I believe BR alerted me to say he couldn't work our case, and by this time, the whole court thing had to be withheld.

PEEKING UNDER THE TENT: Mr. M. Popcorn

I have not one negative thing to say about Mr. Popcorn. When I first started with the district, he and I taught at the same school for several years before I moved on to another building. After some time had passed and I came to J. Austen High School, I was thrilled to be working with him again. I always remembered his great sense of humor. Honestly, if he learned what happened with me at Puzzle City Public Schools, I believe it might disappoint him the way the district worked. His heart was always in the right place and he really cares for the kids. I believe he tried to give them the education they needed. I always felt relaxed with him because he was like that grandfather you always wanted to be close to. I remember having some down days and he could tell right away I wasn't doing well so he always had a quick wit to make me smile. Mr. Popcorn can always brighten your day. I still miss him.

The month of September rolls in with a quirky issue: who's in control of the ship? The reason for the question is, to me, it really seemed like to different conversation between the district and the NEA which took a split between my rep and my lawyer Shelly. Shelly told me she had been in contact with the school district attorney, and that the district lawyer had told Shelly the district was still moving forward with their charges.

However, my rep Ms. Warrior called me a few days later and I emailed Shelly the discussion we had:

"I got a call from (my rep) last night. She told me that Dr. Clown had called her with a new offer. Dr. Clown told (my rep) that she had more power over making negotiations directly with me. The new offer was paying out my contract for this year and signing off on my resignation. The rep and I both thought this offer wasn't enough since we're looking at two years. The

only worry Ms. Warrior had on us seeking a lawsuit was that she understood the district might be close to filing for bankruptcy. I researched that possibility, but what I found was that a school district rarely files for bankruptcy."

[I was correct in that the district never filed for bankruptcy] Ms. Warrior and I had one opinion about what the district should do and the lawyer had her own theory. Shelly felt one year should suffice, but we considered two years was better. Then a few days after this, on August 17th, I received this email from Shelly:

Hi, Xander,

I got a call from the district's attorney this morning. He reiterated their most recent offer to continue to pay your salary and benefits through the end of the 10-11 school year without requiring you to do any work for the district. I asked him about their position on a reference for you and he said they can give only neutral information—dates of employment and salary info—in response to any inquiry. He explained it's the general policy for all employees and that there would be no negative information conveyed to prospective employers. [I underlined that because it will be important later.]

When you and I talked about last week, I told you I thought this was a very good offer. I asked you to consider it and tell me what your final decision might be to settle, assuming that the existing offer would not be enough. When I go back and ask the district for something more, but I need your demands so I can form a negotiating strategy.

You mentioned you were meeting with MI Protection and Advocacy—How did that go?

Let me know if you have questions and call if you want to talk through options. I guess I'd like to go back to them with either acceptance or a counter by the end of this week or early next week.

Thanks,

Shelly

So that happened, but what I need to discuss is the question Shelly asked me in the email about the "Michigan Protection and Advocacy". So there should be one of these in every state. I just want to share with you some things they claim to do on their website and what ultimately happened to me. To begin, here is what our state Protection/Advocacy group states on their website about what their mission is: "To protect the rights of individuals with

disabilities by providing advocacy and legal services."
Doesn't that sound awesome? My lawyer and the
NEA understood so that was why they recommended
I contact them. Here is the profile from the website:

**"Michigan Protection and Advocacy is a federally
mandated system in the state of Michigan which
protects the rights of persons with disabilities
through legally based advocacy. MI P&A
established in 1977 addressed public outcry in
response to the abuse, neglect, and lack of
programming in institutions for persons with
disabilities. MI P&A is the only legal rights
organization in Michigan for people with
disabilities. MI P&A provides nine federally
funded programs to protect the legal rights of
persons with disabilities. Because of limited
funding in each program, the protection and
advocacy system establishes specific service
priorities and objectives annually. MI P&A is a
member of the National Disability Rights
Network (NDRN)."**

Wow… I mean, that really sounds inspiring and I
really couldn't wait until I got their help! (That's
sarcasm, folks.) Let's try to remember, I've been
trying to seek counsel to sue the school district for
discrimination, but I've been having a hard time
finding anyone to take the case. I received a letter on
October 9th and, as you've probably guessed, they
told me they would not offer legal services or any

other services. In the letter, they point out that they have limited resources and I already have counsel and that there were settlement discussions going on with my attorney. Again, the problem is that I wanted to sue the Puzzle City school district and not just take a settlement. I wanted to take them to court! This was just another waste of time. The service is out there to anyone who might need it, but sadly it just didn't work out for me.

Roughly around this same time, my NEA rep Ms. Warrior dropped a bombshell on Gaby and me in this email:

Hey, guys,

I have been moving this week between Puzzle City and Battle Creek, sorry I have been out of touch; it's been somewhat consuming.

Xander, just to clarify, I said I would pitch two years to M. Clown. But assumed we would have to work a compromise in which one year you worked in some capacity of employment, such as an assignment (non-instructional) at the resource center you and Gaby mentioned. I was never sure that the district would "bite" so to speak because we see how PCMI operates.

Sigh.

Ms. A. Warrior

Chapter 6: The Performance Takes A Turn

I learned that my NEA rep was originally from Battle Creek, located just north of Puzzle City. I guess this came as a surprise because she mentioned no move until I got this email. I was sad and angry because it seemed like she abandoned us, but I'm glad she's in a much better place. I understand her being homesick and so she made the move; I would have done the same thing. I still miss her and her counsel. Ms. A. Warrior is fantastic at what she does. I recognize my case was considerably difficult, but she stood up to the challenge.

PEEKING UNDER THE TENT: Ms. A. Warrior

I intently gave the name of my NEA Ms. Warrior for a great reason. A. Warrior is not a tall lady or even menacing; in fact, she was fairly short, with a small frame and blond hair; but don't let that fool you. Ms. Warrior was a gladiator. She really is a person who can be deceived by her looks. As you read in her emails, she can be blunt and caring at the same time. I seemed helpless when she told my wife and me she would move back to her hometown. I realize she had wished for a better result in my case, but dealing with this school district was never easy. I realize what I loved about her the most was that she could always get the answer to questions most reps presumably could not have gotten; for example, finding out about the 'weirdo' comment. I have nothing against her replacement, but she would get the tough information no one else was capable of, and not really caring what position you held in the district.

September was the month that hit me the hardest. During this time, since I was not getting anywhere on the legal front, I turned my attention to as many Aspergers/Autism organizations as I was able to find. Depression seemed to set over me as I turned to organizations like Autism Speaks and Autism Society. I guess I wanted some backup or endorsement for my case. Basically, what I did was email this statement to every foundation:

An Open Letter to all Autistic and Asperger Organizations

I realize you all handle hundreds of thousands of people who either have or are caring for people with autism. The reason I'm writing to you is, something is shaking our rights as disabled people to its core. I have been a teacher for a large school district since 1996. I have never had a reprimand, a professional growth plan, or being removed on administrative leave until this last school year (09-10). I filed my complaint to my State's Human Rights Division, and they did an investigation, but I still haven't heard the results yet. The school district let it made known to me and my NEA rep. that they would fire me no matter what I do to improve back in March 2010. The whole reason they will fire me is that I have Asperger's Syndrome... that's *it. My first clue to this being the case was when the head of HR let my NEA rep learn that the boss ordered her to "**get rid of the weirdo**". So it didn't matter what I did. I was being fired with trumped-up charges so it would look like I was suddenly a bad teacher.*

After having spoken was some attorneys in our area, I'm finding it difficult to find a good representation for my soon ADA case because they told me that ADA cases are very hard to win. I can't believe what I heard that a person being fired because of their disability was more difficult than a racial/gender/age firing! The reason I'm alerting you of this information is that here soon you might see me on your evening news. I really hope I can have the support of your organization behind me because, to be honest, this seriously disturbs me. What does this mean about our right to work without prejudice? What does this say about our defense if someone violates our rights? I suspect I'm not the only one and I'm sure I won't be the last. I seriously doubt this was the vision of what President George H. W. Bush had in mind when he signed the ADA into law.

Thank you for your time.

Xander A. Bell

So, who answered the call? The first email I want to share came from **Autism Speaks**, and what they stated:

Hi Xander – I am so sorry you are having such difficulties and I hope you can get some help.

I would contact JAN hotline for advice: http://askjan.org/

ASK A JAN CONSULTANT

JAN provides free, confidential technical help about job accommodations and the Americans with Disabilities Act (ADA). Send Us Feedback.

Connect with JAN

(800)526-7234 (Voice) (877)781-9403

I am including the Michigan Resource Guide and also information on the protection and advocacy agency in MI.http://www.miadvocacy.org/index.html

* *http://www.miadvocacy.org/Manuals/LegalRights/ Employment.pdf*
* *http://www.autismspeaks.org/resource- guide/state/MI*

I wanted to share these Autism Speaks links about employment rights.

• http://www.autismspeaks.org/docs/family_services_docs/GP_Legal_Guidelines.pdf Employment help starts on page 11

• http://www.autismspeaks.org/sites/default/files/documents/transition/employment.pdf Transition tool kit Employment section

• http://www.autismspeaks.org/family-services/autism-workplace Autism in the workplace. Under Family Services—Basic info, videos, and links to resources and current news.

We also have an adult services portal that has resources for independent living and other resources related to issues facing adults with autism. Plus, you can access our toolkits for adults here:

Transition Toolkit

Employment Toolkit

Housing and Residential Supports Toolkit

Post-Secondary Toolkit

Challenging Behaviors Toolkit

In our resource library, there are links to resources for Adults with Autism, and Asperger's Syndrome.

Employers Guide to Hiring and Retaining Employees with Autism Spectrum Disorders

The employer's perspective on hiring and training adults on the spectrum is another step in our employment initiative. Written from the point of view of an employer that has hired many adults with ASD, we outline steps for employers to use.

Autism in Big Business Report

An expanding roster of large companies across the country that have attempted to publish their inclusion and diversity policies, which include people with developmental disabilities. An explanation of how this fits into the overall employment picture for adults with autism precedes the company's information.

http://autismbeacon.com/topics/articles/employment _support

Good luck Xander. I hope you find the help you need.

Denise Bianchi

Autism Response Team Coordinator

AUTISM SPEAKS

The next organization I heard from was the **Autism Society** and here is what they told me:

Dear Xander,

Thank you for contacting the Autism Society and taking the time to tell your story.

The ADA has regional offices here is the one in your state:

Great Lakes ADA Center

4095 Legacy Parkway, Suite 500 ~ Lansing, Michigan 48911-4264

(800) 949-4232 (V/TTY)

adacenter@michigan.edu

http://www.adamich.org

Each state has federally mandated programs: Protection and Advocacy (P&A) Systems and Client Assistance Programs (CAP) for individuals with disabilities. Collectively, the P&A/CAP network is the largest provider of legally based advocacy services to people with disabilities in the United States. Through training and technical help, legal support, and legislative advocacy, the National Disability Rights Network works to create a society in which it affords people with disabilities equality of opportunity and can fully take part by exercising choice and self-determination.

The National Disability Rights Network serves a wide range of individuals with disabilities including, but not limited to, those with cognitive, mental, sensory, and physical disabilities by guarding against abuse; advocating for basic rights; and ensuring accountability in health care, education, employment, housing, transportation, and within the juvenile and criminal justice systems.

Visit their website at http://www.ndrn.org/en/ndrn-member-agencies.html to find the Protection and Advocacy agency in your state.

Michigan P&A Services

4095 Legacy Pkwy Ste 500

Lansing, MI 48911-4264

P: (517) 487-1755, (800) 288-5923(Voice)

TTY: (517) 374-4687

F: (517) 487-0827

http://www.mpas.org

JAN is also an excellent resource.

The Job Accommodation Network (JAN) is the leading source of free, expert, and confidential guidance on workplace accommodations and disability employment issues. Negotiating toward practical solutions that benefit both employer and employee, JAN helps people with disabilities enhance their employability and shows employers how to capitalize on the value and talent that people with disabilities add to the workplace.

JAN's trusted consultants offer one-on-one guidance on workplace accommodations, the Americans with Disabilities Act (ADA) and related legislation, and self-employment and entrepreneurship options for people with disabilities. Help is available both over the phone and online. Those who can enjoy JAN's services include private employers of all sizes, government agencies, employee representatives, and service providers, and people with disabilities and their families.

JAN represents the most comprehensive job accommodation resource available. From Fortune 500 companies to entrepreneurs, JAN has served customers across the United States and around the world for over 25 years. Its consultants are determined leaders and innovators on disability employment issues, and all have earned at least one Master's degree in their specialized fields, ranging from rehabilitation counseling to education and engineering.

Here is a link to their website:

http://askjan.org/indiv/index.htm#job

(800)526-7234

One more resource:

TASH

1101 15th Street NW, Suite 1212

Washington, D.C. 20005

Call Us: (202) 467-5730, ext. 1309 Call Us: (202) 467-5730, ext. 1309

Website: http://www.tash.org

We hope this information is helpful. For further assistance or clarification of this email, please call the Autism Society's contact center, Autism Source, open seven days a week from 9 a.m. to 9 p.m. at 800-3-AUTISM (800-328-8476).

Sincerely,

Catherine Medovich

Autism Source

Autism Society's Nationwide Contact Center - Providing Information & Referral services to improve the lives of all affected by autism.

I heard from five other organizations but the material that the first two shared was far better than the last five. I just needed to have as much information for anyone who reads this book to have if you or someone you see fall into this struggle. No one, autism or not, should ever have to put up with discrimination in your workplace.

Before I exit from details from September, I wanted to share an excellent letter Shelly wrote to the school district's attorney in response to the district's offer to me. Here is the letter:
Staff Attorney

September 29, 2010

Puzzle City Public Schools Legal Department

Puzzle City, MI

Re: Xander Bell and PCPS

Dear (Staff Attorney),

I am writing to respond to the District's recent offer to continue compensating and paying benefits to Xander Bell as a teacher in the District until the end of the 2010-2011 school year for his resignation effective at the end of this school year and a full release of claims. Outlined in this letter, we believe that the offer does not compensate Mr. Bell for the harm done to him by the District and for the relinquishment of his position as a tenured teacher with the District.

As you understand, Xander Bell has been a teacher in the PCPS since August 1996.

During the first nine years of his tenure with the School District, Mr. Bell successfully taught speech and drama at three different middle schools. In the summer of 2004, they laid him off because of district budgetary issues. He used the 2004-05 school year to get the certification in middle school social studies, increasing his value to the District. In the fall of 2006, he returned to work with the District and joined for the first time at the J. Austen High School. The 2006-2007 school year at JAHS, which is a difficult setting even in the best of times, was utterly chaotic. Among other issues, there was a revolving door in the principal's office with three different individuals serving as principal over the course of the school year. Mr. Bell was assigned to teach high school social studies but then reassigned mid-way through the year to teach middle school students.

While the circumstances are challenging for any teacher, they were especially so for Mr. Bell, who has Asperger's Syndrome and first learned of his diagnosis in (2001). As someone with Asperger's, Mr. Bell is an individual with a disability entitled to the protection of the Americans with Disabilities Act (ADA). Realizing that if he were to continue to perform effectively in the JAHS setting, he would need some accommodations to his disability, Mr. Bell began requesting such accommodations in March 2007. Mr. Bell completed the District's accommodations paperwork, explaining his disability and applying his requested accommodations. After receiving the completed accommodation request, the District sent Mr. Bell from one administrator to another for a period of well over two months.

The District's conduct during this period utterly failed to comply with ADA requirements for the interactive process of determining reasonable accommodations. Despite the bungled handling, the District never showed that Mr. Bell's requested accommodations posed an undue hardship and never showed he would not receive the accommodations he had requested. In August 2007, when Mr. Bell returned to work at JAHS from medical leave, he notified his new principal, Dr. Strongman, that he required accommodations and discussed the specifics of those accommodations.

Mr. Bell taught high school social studies, having got certification to teach that subject in the summer of 2007. Dr. Strongman was supportive of Mr. Bell and the 2007-2008 school year was successful. For the 2008-2009 school year, Mr. Bell taught the American Government for the very first time, besides the American History and World Geography courses, he had taught the previous year. For the 2009-2010 school year, Mr. Bell again taught three different courses at a time, requiring preparation of three entirely different lesson plans — a very heavy load.

Because Mr. Bell's' 2008-2009 American Government students did not perform well on their end-of-course exams (they were far from alone among the District's students), Mr. Bell got put on a Professional Growth Plan in the fall of 2009. This was the first time in his entire 13-year tenure with the District, they had placed him on such a plan. Mr. Bell worked hard on the PGP and made real progress. His students' test scores also improved for the fall 2009 semester. This occurred although the District continually violated Mr. Bell's rights under the ADA by making many unannounced classroom visits in breach of the accommodations Mr. Bell had requested and which the District never disputed.

*In January 2010, Dr. Strongman, who had been overseeing Mr. Bell's PGP, got put on leave in the wake of a series of sexually violent crimes that took place within the school. The administrators who took his place utterly failed not to support Mr. Bell's efforts to satisfy expectations and, in fact, suggested targeting him based on his disability. Astonishingly, one administrator referred offensively to Mr. Bell as **"that weirdo."** Unannounced classroom visits continued, disrupting Mr. Bell's performance. On April 1, Mr. Bell has purportedly issued a Notice of Deficiencies, although the District appears not to have complied with any of the requirements of Section 168.116.2, R.S. MI., starting with the written notice requirement. The District again did not comply with its statutory obligations by failing to "meet and confer" with Mr. Bell as contemplated by statute and Michigan case law; although his PGP was amended to provide for formal observations on 11 dates, they conducted only two of those.*

In summary, not only has the District utterly did not comply with Michigan statutory requirements for terminating a tenured teacher, but even if it had complied with those requirements, Mr. Bell was not incompetent, inefficient, or insubordinate in the performance of his duties. The District has failed to follow its obligations under the ADA. Mr. Bell is a qualified individual with a disability under the ADA and can perform the essential functions of his job with reasonable accommodations. Faced with Mr. Bell's request for accommodations, the District failed to engage in an interactive process with him; such unreasonable delay is itself a violation of the ADA. Then, the District repeatedly and egregiously did not comply with the accommodations Mr. Bell had requested and which his doctors certified were necessary, although the District never showed that those accommodations posed an undue hardship.

In the District's context's unlawful conduct, I summarize only a portion of which in this letter, the District's continued efforts to remove Mr. Bell from his position as a tenured teacher are shocking and we believe they are ultimately unavailing. If the District moved forward with termination charges against Mr. Bell, we are confident that Mr. Bell would prevail in a public hearing before the Board of Education or on appeal to the courts of this state. In addition, Mr. Bell is fully prepared to pursue his claims of discrimination based on disability, seeking actual and punitive damages and attorneys' fees. We are sure that those claims would survive summary judgment and that a jury would have no trouble finding that Mr. Bell's rights got trampled again and again by the District.

While Mr. Bell will contest the District's actions, he understands that doing so will take time and subject him and his family to stress. Therefore, he will consider resolving this matter amicably. However, considering the potential liability the District faces and the damage done to him, we believe the current offer does not compensate Mr. Bell.

We propose that the District continue Mr. Bell on administrative leave, with full pay and benefits, through the end of the 2011-2012 school year. In addition, the District will reimburse Mr. Bell for tuition costs incurred during this 2-year period in pursuit of a Master's Degree, which will assist Mr. Bell in finding subsequent employment. The District will also provide Mr. Bell with a neutral letter of reference and will agree not to challenge any claim he might make for unemployment compensation at the expiration of the 2011-2012 school year. In exchange, Mr. Bell will tender his resignation to be effective at the end of the 2011-2012 school year and will release all claims he may have against the District.

If the District is amenable to a settlement on these terms, please provide me with a draft settlement agreement at your earliest convenience. Please contact me if you wish to discuss any part of this letter.

Truly yours,

Shelly

I really appreciated my lawyer Shelly doing an amazing job, summoning up basically what happened. I realize Shelly and I didn't always agree on the demands, but the letter she wrote was outstanding!

To transition from September to October, I want to share something that was VERY unexpected. As I was emailing all of those organizations, I had an idea. I hoped, well if I would reach out and try to stir the pot, then why not the White House? Yes, I reached the White House's website and emailed **President Barack Obama** to which I sent roughly the same message, but I changed it up to have it addressed more for the president and not just a regular organization. I sent this email on September 8th of 2010... and how did I remember that date? Because on a time-stamped letter dated October 27th, 2010... I received a reply. I truly didn't consider that I would hear a thing, but that's not what happened. The letter was from the U.S. Equal Employment Opportunity Commission Detroit District Office written by JH. Kennedy, the District Director. I'm very proud to share with you the contents of this letter:

U.S. EQUAL EMPLOYMENT OPPORTUNITY COMMISSION

Detroit District Office

Time Stamp: OCT 27 2010

My Address

Dear Mr. Bell:

*This is in response to your email dated September 8, 2010, to **President Obama** concerning the charge of employment you filed with the Michigan Commission on Human Rights against the Puzzle City School District. The President has asked this office to respond directly to you.*

Our records show that you filed a charge of discrimination with the Michigan Department of Civil Rights (MDCR) on June 20, 2010. Under the terms of a work-sharing agreement between MCHR and the Equal Employment Commission (EEOC), MDCR dual-filed your charge with EEOC to protect your federal suit rights, our work-sharing agreement with MDCR provides that the EEOC will not initiate a duplicate investigation of cases being investigated by the MDCR. Consequently, the EEOC will hold your charge of discrimination in suspense pending the completion of MDCR's investigative process. To determine the status of the investigation of your charge, and/or to update MDCR with any additional evidence regarding your charge, you may wish to contact MDCR at the following:

Detroit Service Center - Cadillac Place

3054 West Grand Boulevard, Suite 3-600

Detroit, MI 48202

Phone: 313-456-3700

Fax: 313-456-3701

Toll-Free: 800-482-3604

TTY: 877-878-8464

MDCRServiceCenter@michigan.gov

As you were advised, when the administration process of MCHR has been completed, if you are dissatisfied with the final finding, you may request that the EEOC review MDCR's determination. This is referred to as a substantial weight review. You must make your request for this review, however, in writing within 15 days of your receipt of MDCR's final finding. In this regard, you may contact Mr. J. Wilson, State and Local Coordinator in our Detroit District Office, at the following address:

EEOC

Detroit District Office

Attn: J. Wilson

477 Michigan Ave # 865, Detroit, MI 48226

We hope this information is helpful to you.

Sincerely,

JH. Kennedy

District Director

cc: The White House

Chapter 7: The Clowns Try One Last Laugh

I have to admit this sent me through the moon! [Even though I've had to change all the information, the essence of this letter was real!] Yep! You read that letter right. The President of the United States took a minute and addressed my problem. If the president had an issue, then I have a case! The funny part was before I received this letter there was a developing position that made me downright angry at the time but, in retrospect, had I seen the whole picture, it presumably wouldn't have shocked me. So, I received a call to come to the downtown office for a meeting.

On October 18, 2010, Shelly (who flew in from Detroit) and I drove to the central office for a meeting with Dr. Clown because the school district had decided they would have me do the unthinkable... return. One of my accommodations was having the ability to record any meetings. I would not be a part of it if there were no outlines for the meeting. I still wish that even today having the chance to record the infamous meeting I had back in January with Dr. Ringmaster and the "leadership team", I would give them another, more proper name. I wouldn't let this moment slip by me again. I recorded the whole meeting on my cell phone because since I have Asperger's Syndrome, my memory and being able to recall details of a discussion are nearly impossible for me, so I used my accommodation to record the conference. The room itself was rather uninviting and cold in nature. The wall color was sky blue paneling and industrial framing that one would find a building constructed in the late 50's early 60's. Not quite a cheerful place for a meeting.

Let's play a game. I've written out the dialogue from my recorded meeting. As you read, I would like for you to figure out the motivation behind the meeting. You will be the detective. Do you believe that they called me back because the district really felt bad and wanted me back? Or do you think there is something else more sinister involved?

BEGINNING OF THE TRANSCRIPTION:

Dr. M. Clown enters, and she's not alone. In walks, the school district's attorney, the coordinator Ms. A. Juggler and, yes, Mr. D. Magician strolls the conference room with the rest.

After the introductions, Dr. Clown makes a relatively puzzling omission; "Well Xander, we met a couple of times last year and you had gone through the PGP and the NOD, but what I didn't realize was the administrators had stopped observing you on May 15th and I wasn't aware of it; plus they didn't give you the feedback, so that's our error."

I get it, I get it, you're pondering the same thing I realized — my last observation according to him came on May 15th (which was on a Saturday) from the instructional coach, which made no sense. AND, they admitted to making a mistake?!!!

Dr. Clown declares, "So this is a situation to where we will start again, start clean."

Dr. Clown continues: "Not going into a PGP or a NOD but, returning you to a classroom situation. You will begin observations and within those observations if there are still concerns, then we'll begin the process of the PGP, and if that's not successful, we'll help in intervening and correcting where we see, because last year these were the main two things that didn't happen; and you can correct me if I'm wrong. This is your story."

Whoa! Hmmm, this might be a clue.

"Okay," I responded skeptically.

"Working on student engagement, students being actively engaged in the lesson, not doing other things like sleeping, texting or being on the cell phone. The problem of kids sometimes coming into your room when they weren't supposed to be there and just disrupting the learning environment." Dr. Clown pointedly stated, "And I believe the other piece was classroom management which resulted came up because of that. I believe those were the two key areas that we focused on."

I offered a simple "Hum." But I was thinking to myself, "What is she up too?"

Dr. Clown was good enough to answer my question, "We arranged for you to return to the J. Austen campus and have an assignment that would be the accommodation of American History for high school which you've taught before, and there will be two sections of World History; and we know that's a new curriculum that you haven't taught before."

My stomach went sour in a hurry. Go back to JAHS? I spewed out in my head, She is out of her mind?

"So one reason I asked Ms. Juggler to come to this meeting is that we know we will need to put in some support to help you learn that curriculum and to be prepared and ready for it." Dr. Clown explained.

What I really want to be explained is why Ms. Juggler suddenly became one of my evaluators, I pondered.

Dr. Clown continues, "So our plan and the conversations about the things you feel you need today will be that once we return you to the work environment, we'll give you some time to prepare lessons, to learn curriculum, to learn your routine. If you think it will be beneficial to you, like let's say we do that this week and next week, that first week of school you would co-teach with another teacher because the students will break out into the World History sections, and American History sections are fairly large so the second quarter starts on Monday. We would take a section of 38 kids and make it two sections on 19 kids. So we could spend a week having you co-teach, then get your own room to get you up to speed on the lessons." Dr. Clown dictated. "What do you think about that?"

Let's remember, this was in 2010, and they wanted me to return that same year, teaching a subject I have already taught, yet I felt like they were treating me as either a first-year teacher or one that hasn't been in the classroom for several years. Demeaning? You bet. Nothing like sitting in a room full of 'professional educators' while I get treated like a beginning teacher right out of college.

Shelly observed my bitter reaction to Dr. Clown's proposal and knew she had to step in before I answered that absurd question. "I'm sorry. I'm going to intervene here for a second because I think there are a lot of assumptions in what you just said and I'm not sure if we've gotten to that point yet. I think that obviously, Xander has been through a tremendous ordeal here with the district and he's gone from being a teacher who had many many years of, you know, teaching without incident and being a valued member of the community; to then being under attack, to being placed on leave, to be told he was going to face termination charges, to having a series of offers made to essentially make him go away."

Shelly continued her assault. "To being told now, suddenly, the district is doing an about-face. So I think we need to talk through where that leaves us in terms of his readiness to go jump back into the classroom and for someone with the particular disabilities that he faces, this kind of rapid whiplash of events is very difficult for him to deal with and I think there are several assumptions of what you've laid out in terms of the assignment that we need to unpack and talk through a little bit."

"Sure, we can do that." Dr. Clown was put on her heels.

"And I don't know if you reviewed his accommodation's paperwork recently?" Shelly asked, knowing full well they probably didn't.

"The documents we printed out for everybody." Dr. Clown confirmed.

Shelly plows in, "Okay so you're aware that for him, among the things he needs to help him be successful is he needs stability, he needs consistency, he needs a school environment that is not chaotic and I think what we saw happen at Jane Austen High over those last couple of years was a school environment that was chaotic and devolved into a situation where it became increasingly difficult for Xander to do his job, and that was the context in which he began to receive increased scrutiny of his performance and coupled with that was that the accommodations he requested were not observed or honored."

Shelly pushed through, "So we saw this downward spiral and I think what Xander wants to know, what I need to hear as his advocate is he's going into a situation that is not going to have the chaos, the kind of inconsistency, the kind of unpredictability. I think that only then is that going to be an accommodation that's going to allow him to do the work that needs to be done."

"And that's part of the reason why I want us to meet so he can speak to what has transpired up at Austen High to today." Dr. Clown tried to justify the meeting.

I guess taking a slight shot to his massive ego about the mismanagement under his leadership, Mr. Magician boasted, "So I heard reports when I went into Austen High in the last year that with the two years preceding that moment, you know, some things you described."

"Right." Shelly wasn't convinced.

Mr. Magician tries to correct the perception, "I've heard other reports and such, but I believe that at the end of the year we created that consistency and stability in the environment with the expectations for staff and students. And I've been out to J. Austen about four times this year and that same tone, that same environment has continued under the leadership of Mr. Purple [the new principal to take over from Mr. Magician so he might go back to his other duties]. It's not perfect, but I can tell that they picked up that baton where we ended so it has not reverted to old ways, so the staff is working well. There are also quite a few new teachers out there, but they're working together well, so there are enough veterans there that still remember Mr. Bell to make the introductions through their PLC (Professional Learning Circles) time and so forth."

Mr. Magician directly addressed me: "You probably know more of the specific teachers. [The department chair] is still there with social studies, I don't remember what other turnovers they may have had in that department, but there is a team of teachers you would be familiar with. I believe that would allow for that environment you're seeking. Then in terms of the advanced notice of observations, I don't see that as being an issue, I didn't know about that last year either, but we can give Mr. Purple [new principal] that notice and if there are any other written accommodations that Mr. Purple can provide that would make even more clear for him."

Shelly clarified: "What I'm hearing though is that this was a school that I think is widely acknowledged had really gone to the tank; I mean there was a real understanding that the school was in deep trouble. What I'm hearing you say is that at the end of the year, there was a plan that was put into place and here we are in mid-October, two months into the school year already in progress. That doesn't sound to me like a school that is consistent and a relatively effective calm environment for someone with Xander's particular disabilities, and that is the concern."

"The district lawyer and I talked about the fact that you guys were talking about putting him back at J. Austen High. I expressed concern to the district lawyer about that because you learned our experience was that this school was not a good working environment for someone with Xander's particular issues. I think the district has other school environments that are more mature in terms of leadership and consistency. It's a more mature situation, there's been more time for that environment to grow and flourish. What you're talking about at J. Austen sounds to me like it's still in its infancy and I realize how long it takes a school culture to turn around. I know how many years, even of good consistent leadership, it takes for a real school culture to turn around. My concern is not the description of J. Austen High at the moment right now. I have very serious concerns about putting him back into that contest." Shelly states bluntly.

Mr. Magician backpedaled: "If I may. I wanted to add that when I say it's not perfect, I don't want to paint the picture that it is chaotic. It's not chaotic, it's an environment where I walk through and the students are orderly, cordial and quiet. I see when I walk through the cafeteria that students are finishing up their lunch in and waiting for adults to dismiss the table. That was a change I made last year. I see those same things, those expectations are clear for students. It is a much-improved environment; in fact, I have had several teachers come to me and say that things are going well. This is coming from teachers, but the main point I want to bring up is that this is an urban environment and so we have a superintendent who's in his third year. I know many of the surrounding areas that have them for 10 to 15 years in that place."

Mr. Magician suddenly forgets that he's the head of the leadership for the district and makes this sudden omission about his job to train and keep leaders in buildings without having a lot of turnovers. "J. Austen has a new leader, but out of our eight high schools, six are on their first or second year in that building. So new leadership will be consistent and with two new middle schools that just came open and those two are in their first year there, so out of ten secondary schools eight of the ten have new leadership so we will not find these very opportunities for this environment that you seek that goes along with the system in urban education you hoping to get for Mr. Bell's request ..."

Once again, Mr. Magician directed his comments at me, "...and whenever, and I'm uncertain how long, you, Mr. Bell, have worked for the district, but when we come into an urban environment that comes with the territory, you know that, so we will not find necessarily what I hear you or heard you describe is consistent with every other teacher that applies with the Puzzle City Public Schools when they walk into our schools, and that is something we build and work toward a perfect end together. We can't expect to walk into that perfect scenario."

Shelly was alert to Mr. Magician's faux pas and said, "I understand what you're saying and I hear there will be *turnover* in leadership, but think some situations and schools were already fairly even keel, fairly decent trajectory and here you are talking about a school that was not. You have a new leader coming into a situation like that and I think it's that combination of a school that was in trouble with new leadership. That's great and I'm glad to hear that it seems to be on a positive path, but my concern is that we're not there yet."

Mr. Magician using bullying tactic: "And that's why I wanted to bring up those other leaders that we have seven other schools the size of J. Austen High that is in the same situation, and Mr. Bell will be in there again, a school where they're about creating improvement as a cohort, and that same expectation I would believe falls on Mr. Bell along with the other teachers at J. Austen, along with the other schools. They are building new programs essentially."

Shelly brushed off the babbling. "And that's terrific, but what I'm wondering is, Was there any consideration to alternate replacement?"

Mr. Clown answered, "We allow the building principal to select their own hires, so we tend not to force assignments on them and cause disruptions, so going back to J. Austen makes sense, and it seems like the appropriate place. Some good things are familiarity, routines, and colleagues that can be a beneficiary."

Shelly not impressed: "Familiarity is great if that's a positive thing, but I think in these instances it may not be positive. I think there was an awful lot of bad stuff that happened there and I think the familiarity of that occasion is problematic in this case. And what you say about 'principals making their own hires and something you rarely force', I understand that, but the ADA allows you to do things outside of your normal policy to make accommodations."

"Sure. And we can make the accommodations as we did at J. Austen, it's just that this was the placement the administration approved of." Dr. Clown states.

Shelly attempts to ease the discussion. "I understand that you know this is a conversation. This is an interactive process, the magic words, and you understand we have very serious concerns about that particular building, that particular environment as a place that will accommodate him."

"We hear them." Dr. Clown said flatly.

Shelly was now confused. "Okay?"

District Lawyer attempts to break the standoff. "I suppose you all might want some time to have you and Xander discuss this."

"I mean it sounds to me like a take it or leave it," Shelly said, forcing the issue. "Is that what I'm hearing?"

Clown sounded startled, "Well, no, as you made mention this is an interactive process, but things that you're describing that we don't need a different placement what Mr. Magician is referring to we have issues all over our schools so we really believe this is the best placement to provide the greatest stability and support, the familiarity, the routines, the size of the school and the stability that it has from last Spring until now."

Shelly was diplomatic: "One option we discussed is what about GR. Ford High School? And another one we talked about was North West High, oh sorry, I meant West High? I mean, either of those seems to be schools that have a more established culture."

Dr. Clown openly ponders, "We won't be looking at Ford because we've gone down in student enrollment there because right now, we have the best student/teacher ratio sitting at Ford, so we don't have a need for a teacher. **West?** Well, I guess it's something we can consider."

Suddenly, Dr. Clown's consideration quickly summoned the astonished faces of Ms. Juggler, Mr. Magician, and the lawyer, as if this would not be part of the plan.

Dr. Clown continued ignoring their bewilderment. "They have had an increase in enrollment, but I can't guarantee you would be back in the American history curriculum. We have to talk to Mr. T. Sideshow about his needs because this is what we asked for Austen High in trying to come up with this assignment — to address those needs because it has to be about efficiency for ourselves."

Dr. Clown turned to me, "So are you concerned about the stress of going into a completely new environment, a high school with almost 1000 students as opposed to 450 in your building?"

I addressed the question, "From what I've heard from West, I know they've done some excellent things. I've known Mr. Sideshow in the past."

This was my chance to shut down Mr. Magician's bullying for good. I confidently shot back. "Just to address your question, I started in 1996, so yeah, I've been in the district for a while."

Not even waiting for a smug response, I enlightened Dr. Clown, "I've had colleagues go over to West and observed the building and how well managed it was last year. Mr. Sideshow has been there for six years?"

Dr. Clown, looking astonished, said, "Yes."

"That's the reason I brought this school up for Shelly and me."

"Your deal with the larger population and the complexities of the inner mixing of students. Do you have any experience on the ELL (English Language Learners) side?" Dr. Clown questioned.

"Only I had to deal with the sign language at my old school. I've dealt with all kinds of languages and it doesn't bother me. I was in North West for summer school."

"You said you were at North West?"

"Yes, I did some summer teaching over there. I've been here since 1996. I've seen everything. I mean I've literally been through everything."

(This evoked a laugh from the group.)

In conclusion, I said, "I don't think there's not a thing I haven't experienced yet." I stated this, knowing that North West was central for several ethnicities all going to that school.

Shelly tests, "I get the impression that's less of a concern the educational environment, the teaching morale and the supportiveness of the climate overall. I think he's got the climate he needs to work in, he's a very experienced and accomplished teacher. I think given that he will excel."

Dr. Clown was double-checking, "So from a range of looking at issues then, that meant you were into moving from one crowd to another and you had time to prepare for the change we're looking at?"

I said, "I think it's possible."

"Okay."

"Let me just note one thing about this whole PGP in the first place, and you may not realize this, but this whole thing started because of my American government scores my first year teaching [the subject] ever came back terrible. They put me on a PGP to help me raise them up. Ms. Juggler put in what I thought was a very good system to do this the best that I can and Mr. Popcorn, God bless the man, came in and tried to help too."

I turn to Ms. Juggler as I try to pull her into the conversation. "Is it a full year now?"

Ms. Juggler shyly, "Yes, it's a full year now."

Frustrated, I just laid it all out, "This whole situation started with one man, and it just snowballed, rolling down the hill as it started to pick up steam, gathering more issues as it rolled thus the impact hit with a crushing blow. It was a horrible thing that really hurt many people. I mean it damaged a lot of lives. People that I call friends, people that I want to call friends; I mean it hurt. It forced many people to do things they probably didn't want to do. And so going back it almost seems like we're just throwing another log on the fire and for me, that's why I cringed when she [Shelly] told me about going back to J. Austen. I ask,

'Are you serious?' I mean, you just kind of blew my mind."

Shelly doing damage control: "I think what I'm hearing in our conversations before that having a fresh start after everything that's happened and how this was handled by the district for those months and mishandled frankly, that having a fresh start in a new climate that is more supportive is essential to a forward-moving success."

Dr. Clown sets the parameters, "So Xander, in wanting to be a supportive climate if you want to you can have a conversation with Mr. Sideshow before going then I think that is an option on the table so you are going in like an interview if he senses that this isn't a good fit."

Myself in defense, "I'll be glad to talk to Mr. Sideshow. I think my wife would like it. She knows Mr. Sideshow really well."

"Well, that's something we can consider."

Shelly supports, "I think that's a very smart idea. And you mentioned two new preps?" (Preps are the different courses that are taught for a teacher.)

"I'm not sure what West needs." "It was that J. Austen needed American History and World History." "So we don't know until you meet with Mr. Sideshow and see if this is a possibility, then if it is, what does West need? It might turn out it's the same thing; it may be all American history; it might be different preps."

Shelly turns to me to ask: "You taught some other things other than American history. Haven't you?"

"Oh yeah. We mentioned American government, World geography, Psychology/Sociology - that was so much fun, I really enjoyed that."

"So there's some flexibility in there in terms of his experience."

"I've run the gambit. They had expanded my role; it was nice."

I said to Ms. Juggler again, "There was that time I taught Economics for a little while. Remember that?"

"Yeah."

"Is that still a semester class?"

"Yeah, it's still a semester."

I wasn't able to get her to open up. I was really hoping for at least some comments about the chaos last year.

Shelly observes, "I think the key there is enough time to prepare to get himself up to speed with the new curriculum. One challenge he faced, I forget which school year it was, but there was the one year you had three different courses to prepare lessons for at the same time, and one or two of those were new."

I stated, "Well, that was last year." "I mean it's not impossible, you just have to be ready for it. Yes granted, probably not ideal, but when I heard Psychology/Sociology, I thought this would be interesting. It was only one class, but it wasn't too bad. The classes flip-flopped with another teacher. So I worked a lot."

Dr. Clown redirected, "No matter the role, what are the other accommodations?"

END OF THE TRANSCRIPTION

The conversation changed to what you have already read previously. The meeting seemed to cover two main topics, my placement, and my accommodations. So detectives, what do you think? Was this a legitimate we're taking you back, or we screwed up and we need a redo on your firing? I'm willing to bet you already identified the answer.

Later in that meeting, Dr. Clown goes on to note how I would be better with older students as I stated it in my accommodations. I told her that middle school was out of the question, but freshman might be a possibility. Shelly walked the administrators through a document that given around that came from the JAN (Jobs Accommodations Network) people. She pointed out specific things like unannounced visits, dramatic changes, and chaotic situations. I honestly felt like they really didn't care. We took about a ten-minute break and Shelly and I reflected on what had transpired. Shelly and I agreed that the whole idea of going back to J. Austen HS was out. We had a good notion about West High School and the potential they had since my wife worked with the principal. I voiced my concern about how Dr. Clown had made it appear I would really get that 'fresh start' but, I had told Shelly that I really didn't buy it.

Nothing said in that meeting appeared like I had the guaranteed job security. The discussion sounded like we're just bringing you back to fire you again; because I remember what I stated earlier about the cost. After the break, only Dr. Clown and I believe the attorney returned. I asked Dr. Clown a question about where she came from, which was a college town in central Michigan. Dr. Clown disclosed to me she was looking to return to her hometown once retiring which I guessed would be considerably soon but no real time table is given. We wrapped the meeting, and we decided I would be with a state advocate, Vicki, who was friends with Gaby and me. We would arrange a meeting to meet with Mr. Sideshow the principal at West High School.

Chapter 8: No Need For A Sequel

Let me take a minute to explain the whole GR. Ford school controversy. Some school districts have a 'special' school for those students who show highly intellectual skills in different areas of education. Not just any student enters those hallowed walls of a school where students must test and picked by a panel to attend that school. GR. Ford was the PCPS's crown jewel. They accepted only the students that not only showed excellence in the classroom but likewise exhibit excellence in everything else. If a student jeopardizes their education with horrible grades or behavior, they would move them to a different school in the district and finish out their time in their new surroundings. Shelly and I both considered GR. Ford had the best potential for me to land; even the NEA rep fought to get me moved there when this whole fiasco blew up back in January. The ironic thing was HR kept saying that there was no position available at GR. Ford, but this happened:

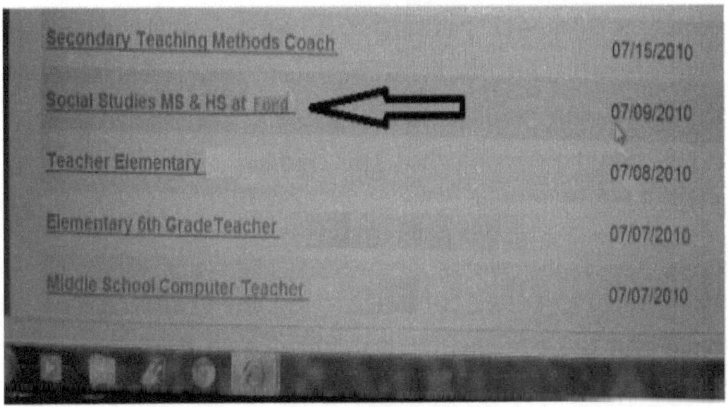

Four days later on October 22nd, 2010, my advocate Vicki and I met with Mr. T. Sideshow, Ms. S. Fortune-Teller vice-principal and Ms. M. Trick-shot was the ADA person out of the district's HR. In this meeting, they wanted to learn my accommodations and how I was as a teacher. The first thing they pushed was my classroom discipline. Once again, I got slammed with that first-year teacher mentality as they belittled my professionalism. This whole discussion took approximately twenty minutes, and I was getting frustrated because they were pressing the accommodations that weren't a general issue.

They wanted to play the 'what if game' just to see what an Aspie teacher might do in different scenarios. I took this cross-examining as an attack. I finally had to remind them that the conditions in the room I can always handle the distractions outside of the room were the real problem. Mr. Sideshow seemed like they would accommodate most of my disabilities but not all. To me, this wasn't too big of a concern. The vice-principal, however, was considerably harsh. First, Ms. Fortune-Teller started throwing out scenarios one after another, not even bothering to recall what she had already stated.

Ms. Fortune-Teller then attacked the controversy with change by stating that "you're coming into the middle of the school year and I must yank students out of classes that might have been their favorite teacher and place them into your class with them not knowing who you are."

As the meeting moved along, Mr. Sideshow had to leave the meeting and only Ms. Fortune-Teller stood alone from the West administration. The discussion ran fairly well until right at the end, and suddenly Ms. Fortune-Teller started to echo much of the same language as Dr. Clown did. "I just want you to meet your job description and if you're not meeting your job description, that's where, you know, we'll be looking at making sure you have the support but, at some point we have to say okay we need to decide because we provided the support, you understand, and you're not meeting your job description. We've already gone over this; we've given you some strategies. We modeled it for you. We brought you in."

Ms. Fortune-Teller concludes, "So that's where my concern comes in about the change."

Ms. Fortune-Teller looked to lay out the idea that headhunting and the standing order of the "***get rid of the weirdo***" showed to still be in play. One other note about this meeting, I made a mention about the age of the students, at the time they told me that their greatest need was the freshman World History and sophomore American History courses. The meeting concluded the understanding that I had to meet with my NEA people and Ms. Trick-shot had to speak with Dr. Clown and her HR folks.

Gaby and I finally got to meet our new NEA rep on October 25th. I'll call him Kenny. I identified he was walking into a relatively difficult case because just two days before we met. I received a letter in the mail from the Human Resource Department with my new orders. There was a letter and a memo from Dr. Clown. This is what the letter said:

Dear Mr. Bell:

Your placement effective October 31, 2010, and for the rest of the 2010-2011 school year is given below. While on this assignment, you will maintain your full benefits and your teacher salary.

Location: WEST HIGH SCHOOL

Position: SOCIAL STUDIES TEACHER

Please contact your supervisor for the specific assignment, grade level, or content area information. The District reserves the right to change assignments based on student and/or programmatic needs.

Sincerely,

Dr. M. Clown

The big topic that received the great debate about the most when the accommodations addressed and the school district was directly challenging them. When the proposed draft for my return came forward, the main issue was in questioning the accommodations as 'reasonable'. Understand that any place of employment can only in here to the ADA law by defining what reasonable accommodations are and is it possible for the employer to offer them. If you recall, I provided the list of accommodations I had requested to the district but, since that was several pages back here was the list again:

• Remove or reduce distractions from my classroom.

• Supply proper working equipment and office supplies.

• Provide specific feedback to help employee target areas of improvement. (Things possible with my disability.)

• Provide written instructions. (That includes meeting notes; if not, then recording devices is used.)

• Prompt me with verbal cues.

• Allow additional training time for new tasks. (if I consider it's needed.)

• Identify areas of improvement for an employee in a fair and consistent manner.

• Give adequate notice of any changes or meetings. (This included any person wanting to enter the classroom for any reason because this ties into the first accommodation.)

Now let me share with you a terrific definition of "Reasonable Accommodation" from the source The ADA website:

"REASONABLE ACCOMMODATION is any change to the application or hiring process, to the job, to the way the job outlined, or the work environment that allows a person with a disability who is qualified to perform the essential functions of that job and enjoy equal employment opportunities. We consider accommodations 'reasonable' if they do not create an undue hardship or direct threat."

So I ask you as the reader, of these eight simple requests, would you consider any of them to be an "undue hardship or a direct threat"? I did not have one lawyer, adviser, building administrator tell this was the case. I can honestly understand if there were, in fact, ridiculous requests but if you can get the chance to check out the website as good examples of proper requests. This leads me to this memo from the school district.

Here is the memo that spelled out specifically what I was to do and what my duties entail at West High School:

Re: Return to Work

As you experienced, we met on Monday, October 18th, 2010 to discuss your return to work. We had arranged for you to return to a position at JAHS teaching American History at the middle and high school level. During the process of our discussion, you asked for an assignment at another school. West High School discussed the current enrollment there has increased.

We set up a meeting for you on Friday, October 22nd, 2010 with Mr. Sideshow, Principal at West, to discuss a

158

position and review necessary accommodations. Based upon this discussion, we have submitted a teaching position for you at West High School starting Monday, October 31th, 2010.

Today, October 27th, 2010 your attorney informed us that because of your wife's surgery this week [Gaby was having wires running up her back to help with her pain] they need you for her care until October 31st, 2010. As planned, we have formally reinstated your employment as of October 31, 2010, and we will approve the FMLA (Family Medical Leave Act) leave for October 31st, 2010 - November 3rd, 2010. The meeting to review your transition plan will now be Monday, November 8th, 2010 at the Board of Education at 8:00 AM with Ms. Trick-shot instead of October 31st, 2010. After this meeting, you will go to West High School.

To facilitate a successful transition for you, I am outlining the position and accommodations discussed up to this point. Ms. Trick-shot will meet with you on Monday, November 8th, 2010 at 8:00 AM at the Central Office to discuss this plan and once again review the accommodations with you to decide if you have any additional needs or suggestions. After the meeting, you will then officially report at West High School. While you are at the Board of Education on November 8th, 2010, we will also make you a new name badge and have you go through the technology department to be sure your laptop is ready for use.

Dr. Clown will outline times, grade, subject, and other things included. I will give my own comments on how this memo passed against several of my accommodations. When I first got this memo attachment, I expected this to be a joke. I thought like all those meet and all that time I spent explaining my condition and the accommodations just fell on deaf ears:

During the week of November 8th - November 12th, 2010, you will have time to prepare lessons, and shadow teachers to learn the expectations and routines of West High School. [14 years in the school district, 4 different schools and they wanted me to follow teachers around to learn the high school routines. As a professional, I can't tell you how insulting this would be.]

The week of November 15th to November 19th, 2010, you will co-teach in the curriculum to which you would replicate. [Again, more professional insults, I had already taught the subject for four years when I returned to the school district.]

Starting on November 22nd, 2010, you will assume your own classes.

West High School: School day operates as follows for the week:

Monday to Friday 7:20 AM from 2:20 PM

The teachers at West have also been meeting in their content area or professional learning communities one day a week voluntarily. This teacher-led meeting has been very beneficial for teachers.

Your teaching assignment will be:

1st - 5th Period: 8th grade

6th Period: Conference/Plan Time

7th Period: 8th grade

[You read that right. Middle School, the one thing I was never to teach again. I was not ready to hop on this bandwagon!]

Mr. Sideshow shared with me you already discussed the assignment because this is where the need exists at West to best serve our students. [Bull Crap! We never discussed middle school. The only time we mentioned it when they stated... they had said the eighth grade... that was it.]

One teacher preparation is usually not the norm as you notice; However, this will assist you in your transition. [Indeed, Dr. Clown was wrong (again), all teachers had at least one plan time.]

The accommodations you have requested which we have addressed. [Not!]

**Assignment at a different school rather than JAHS.*

**Assignment will be at West.*

**Advance notice of expectations and observations.*

Delivering Mr. Bell his assignments in writing today.

Developing a week of planning and opportunity to shadow fellow teachers so he can develop lessons and get acclimated to the operations of West High School. [This was NOT one of them! I did not need my handheld!]

When Mr. Bell has a scheduled observation, we will inform him in advance.

Mr. Bell should also prepare for weekly unscheduled observations, as this is an ongoing part of a teacher's expectations. [Violates my accommodations.]

We will provide Mr. Bell with notes from all observations.

Advanced notice of meeting topics: We will inform Mr. Bell before what the meeting will be.

*Assignment teaching 10th to 12th grade students.

Mr. Bell's assignment fit with his certification, the needs of our students, and his transition as the three main priorities.

During the conference with Mr. Sideshow, the needs of West students were a primary focus and the possibility your assignment might exist as six sections of 8th grade Social Studies versus upper grades. [And that was their best excuse why I got stuck with the worst condition at West H.S.]

*Forbidding students from bringing cellphones in the classroom.

Mr. Bell has stated that he can maintain control in his classroom. The administration will support Mr. Bell as he follows the protocols set up to deal with students who bring inappropriate items into the classroom and distract from learning.

+ 1st - Address expectations with the students.

+ 2nd - Contact the Parent.

+ 3rd - Call the administrator for help. [I mean because I don't understand how to manage a class with students and cell phones... (sarcasm)]

Mr. Bell agreed that this would help him. [Another slap in the face...thank you.]

*Preventing students from gathering in the hallway outside his door where he is teaching.

Students at West High School should not be in the hallways unless they have a pass for a specific purpose.

This has not been a problem at West High School. [Sure it hasn't...not.]

[The next thing on the memo was a bullet point of the duties and responsibilities of the teacher...You got that right...they are telling me, a veteran teacher of 14 years in THEIR district alone, how to do my job. This is a great example of how a job can truly demean a professional person.]

The essential duties and responsibilities of the teacher include:

• Instructs students by lecturing, showing, and using audiovisual aids and other materials to supplement presentations.

• Prepares course objectives and outline for the course of study, following curriculum guidelines or requirements of state and school.

• Assigns lessons and corrects homework.

• Administers test pupil progress, record results, and issue reports informing parents of progress.

• Keeps an attendance record.

- *Maintains discipline in the classroom.*

- *Meet with parents to discuss student progress and problems.*

- *Takes part in faculty and professional meetings, educational conferences, and teacher training workshops.*
- *Performs related duties such as sponsoring one or more activities or student organizations, assisting pupils in selecting the course of study, and counseling students in change and academic problems.*

This letter outlines your duties to assist you by providing to you in writing a clear plan for your transition and what to expect while outlining the accommodations you have requested and how we have addressed them. [No... they just made it worse.]

Your meeting with Ms. Trick-shot on Monday, November 8th, 2010, at 8:00 AM will give you an opportunity to respond to this letter or you may do so through your attorney before then if you desire.

Our intent is to support you for a successful transition as you return to a teaching position. Attached is your placement letter and FMLA paperwork for your leave for October 31, 2010, to November 3, 2010. Should you need additional leave, we will assist you.

Attached was a Family Medical Leave Act form filled out, at least most of it was for me. So everything looked in order except for one problem for the school district... I filed a complaint with the Human Rights people. During the entire time, I was communicating with the district on how they suddenly wanted to bring me back. I had likewise been emailing a member of the Michigan Department of Civil Rights (MDCR). The unit supervisor of the MDCR had been asking questions about if we (the district and myself) had come to a compromise. I had told her about the meetings we had. This is what I told the supervisor:

I apologize about the slight tardiness of my update to you about the two meetings that I had on Monday, Oct. 18, which was at the board building and the second meeting was on Friday, Oct 22 at West High School. What I have provided was a sound clip from both meetings I recorded (which is one of my ADA accommodations since there was no scribe) and the written transcript of this dialogue.

The first meeting had Dr. Clown (Head of HR), Social Study Coordinator Ms. Juggler, Mr. Magician (Head of Leadership and interim principal at J. Austen HS), the PCPS district lawyer, my NEA lawyer Shelly and myself. The sound clip comes from the very beginning of the meeting. As you read, you apparently note that at no time did Dr. Clown ever admit that the error from the district was because they didn't accommodate for my Asperger's, instead they blame it on procedural errors of getting me fired. The only reason they want to put me back to work was to make sure they can fire me the correct way!

The second meeting had Mr. Sideshow (Principal of West HS), Ms. Fortune-Teller (Vice-Principal of West HS), Ms. Trick-shot (ADA coordinator for the district), Vicki (State Family Support Coordinator and Autism Navigator/my advocate) and myself. My first reflection when I met Ms. Trick-shot was 'why weren't you at the meeting on Monday?' So I asked her and her answer was 'I just go where they tell me.' The meeting was more of an evaluation to test West HS on whether they might support my ADA accommodations. To me, it sounded like the answer was 'yes' sometimes and 'no' on others. The sound clip comes toward the very end of the meeting where it implied Ms. Fortune-Teller made it obvious on my future if I come to West HS. Not too inviting.

So the unit supervisor contacted the school district to find out what to do. I was in contact with the NEA to see if the investigation should move forward. I will let the investigation continue, and the district wanted to meet to negotiate my complaint. I had spoken with a member of JAN so I shared that information with the MDCR about that discussion:

We spoke with the people from JAN and we just realized this:

During the week of March 1-5, my NEA Rep. had advised me to go online and fill out a request for a voluntary transfer. I realized that my time would be up at J. Austen and Dr. Clown of HR and the NEA Rep sensed I needed a change of location, especially with all the problems at JAHS. I did, in fact, fill out the request form. I told later that they would fire me from the district no matter how well I did in the classroom. At the end of May, they put me on administrative leave pending my firing. When summer came, I still didn't get fired, but my wife noticed that GR. Ford HS had an opening for a high school Social Studies teacher and my wife commented: "that it was too bad that they want to fire you because the district has just the job for you and didn't you ask for a transfer there, anyway?"

My wife even took a picture of the job to prove there was an opening. (see previous photo) Summer turns into fall and still no firing, but they make an offer for me to return to the classroom. The school district claims that I can't go to GR. Ford HS because they had filled the position, but my ADA accommodations would have been best suited at GR. Ford High School and now the district doesn't imply to expect they have an obligation to place me there. I filled out a voluntary request form for a transfer way before they placed the new teacher. The people at JAN informed me that the district violated my ADA rights when I wasn't able to transfer to GR. Ford, which all involved perceived that GR. Ford H.S. was the best placement for me. The district didn't put me there because they don't care about ADA accommodations and needing to do what's best for the employee. Now they want to place me at a high school teaching eighth-graders in which my doctors specifically stated that working with older high school students is best for me. I have taught 10-12th grades in the past. Now that I won't go along with their plans, first my resigning and taking a package arrangement, truly an insult to me as a teacher. I still think this might be my retribution for filing a complaint with the Michigan Department on Civil Rights.

On October 28th, the unit supervisor told me that the district wanted to go into mediation I assumed that was fine. Vicki pointed this out in an email with the arrangement for my return: "I see it's all just a smoke screen to pretend they are accommodating you. So you will decline the crazy offer- then they can proceed." Vicki saw right through the clown. "What they really want to do is fire you."

Chapter 9: The Final Curtain Call

THIS WAS THE SERIES OF CORRESPONDENCE ABOUT THE MEDIATION

Me: "When do you expect mediation taking place? Who's involved in the mediation? Where would this take place?"

Unit Supervisor: "It typically takes a few weeks to get our cases assigned to a mediator, and the mediator contacts the parties to schedule the mediation at a mutually convenient time. Some mediators use their own offices in the Puzzle City area, and others use state facilities in the East Bottoms of the Puzzle City downtown area. Parties have occasionally agreed to meet at the office of one attorney. Typically, the parties, their representative(s), and the mediator are involved. If you have particular concerns about the participants, date, or location, you can work through it with the mediator when contacted."

Kenny NEA Rep: "Thank you for the information. I am a representative with Michigan NEA and will attend the mediation. I will be out of the country from November 16 to December 3. I will be back in the office on Monday, Dec 5th. I wanted you to have my schedule prior to the scheduling of this mediation."

I'm sure you're perhaps guessing what does that matter? Well, that explains why I never had that meeting with HR about the 8th grade Social St. job at West High School. Because the mediation needed resolution before I would ever come back. Since Kenny would be out until early December and the MDCR had to finish their investigation, I had to sit at home and I really didn't mind. Going back and teaching middle school did not sit well with me at all, and I honestly believe the district recognized that.

Now I want to take a moment to share with you the discussion that my NEA lawyer had with the district lawyer about the meeting about my return to work. Let's just say my lawyer Shelly was about as impressed as I was:

District Lawyer: "Attached are five documents regarding Mr. Bell's placement at West, ADA accommodations, and paperwork to be filled out and returned about Mr. Bell's request for FMLA leave. I do not have an email address for Mr. Bell. If you have an email address for him and can provide it, I can send this to his email directly or would appreciate it if you would forward it to him. I will put it in the mail to him today. If he has questions on the FMLA paperwork, please have him contact Ms. Trick-shot in the HR Department. He needs to return the paperwork to Ms. Trick-shot by November 5, 2010."

"I would appreciate it when you speak with Mr. Bell that you inform him of the new date for the meeting with HR to review his placement at West High School is Monday, November 8, 2010, at 8:00 am. He is to report to the Human Relations Department on the 13th floor of the Board of Education Building for his meeting."

Please call or email with questions.

Shelly NEA Lawyer: "I would like to discuss a couple of points in the district's proposed draft for Xander Bell's return to work. There may be additional items that Xander will address directly with Ms. Trick-shot on November 8th, but these are the things I am most concerned about."

"Foremost, we are shocked and dismayed that the district would see fit to assign Mr. Bell to teach 6 sections of 8th graders — the youngest students at West High School and well outside the grade 10-12 range that Mr. Bell's doctors have shown is necessary to accommodate his disability. My request earlier today for you to identify any other vacant positions to which Mr. Bell may be assigned is a direct response to the impropriety of the grade-level assignments proposed in this arrangement. Further, contrary to the assertions on page 2 of the plan, there was NO discussion about teaching 8th graders when Mr. Bell met with West HD administrators and Ms. Trick-shot on October 22nd. The lowest grade level discussed was 9th and then in the difficulties Mr. Bell experiences in teaching such young students. Such a blatant misstatement does nothing to inspire confidence in the district. While I appreciate that teaching 6 sections of the same class would lighten the preparation burden for Mr. Bell, any benefit from that would be utterly negated by the age group of the students he would be teaching. In this area of his accommodations, the district needs to do better."

"Second, I am unaware of any evaluation protocol for teachers that would require weekly unscheduled observations, absent the presence of deficiencies or a PGP, both of which we have agreed are not applicable here as Mr. Bell is starting with a clean slate. Thus, there should be no need for Mr. Bell to be prepared for weekly unscheduled observations and we stand by the position that it is the reasonable accommodation that does not pose an undue hardship for the district to provide 24-hour minimum advance notice prior to all observations in Mr. Bell's classroom."

"Even if unscheduled weekly observations are "an ongoing part of the teacher's expectations", which we do not believe they are, it is entirely appropriate to adjust that policy for a teacher with a disability if doing so allows him to perform the essential functions of his job. There is nothing in the list of essential functions that suggests being able to tolerate unscheduled and unannounced weekly observations is an essential function of Mr. Bell's job and the district has other equally effective ways of evaluating his performance that will not disrupt his ability to work unscheduled observations do. Also, references to "advance notice" of observations and they should adjust meeting topics to provide more specificity and allow for at least 24 hours' notice."

"Finally, regarding meetings of any sort with administrators, Mr. Bell requires either a scribe/note-taker or permission to record so he can review and process information and feedback he is receiving from the district. We need to have that included in the return to work plan."

"Please let me know if you have questions about these items. I would like to see a revised draft of the plan before Xander meets with Ms. Trick-shot on November 8th, if at all possible."

Thanks.

District Lawyer: "Prior to the discussion regarding placement of Mr. Bell at West they had discussed it that there was a place at JAHS to teach 9th and 10th grade World and American History. Is that something he would consider?"

"Please call or email me with your response."

Shelly, NEA Lawyer: "No, as was discussed on the 18th, JAHS poses a different set of problems regarding Mr. Bell's accommodations. You should realize in early March of this year when it became increasingly clear that Mr. Bell cannot be accommodated at JAHS, Dr. Clown proposed that Mr. Bell should explore a transfer to another school and he did, in fact, complete a voluntary transfer request.

Had that request been honored during that time or even in the summer, I suspect the record would reflect that there were a variety of open positions into which he might have transferred that would have provided him with the accommodations he needs. Instead, the district undertook a bungled and unlawful campaign to get rid of him and filled those positions, including at least one for a social studies teacher at GR. Ford Prep, with other teachers. It is patently offensive and, I would argue, a perpetuation of the district's discriminatory conduct, for the district to claim that it has no other options for his placement when that condition exists (to the extent it does) because of the district's own unclean hands."

Thanks.

District Lawyer: "Thank you for your email. Will you please notify Mr. Bell that he need not report to the Human Resources Department at the Board of Education Building on Monday, November 8, 2010, at 8:00 a.m. as previously directed?"

"This will allow PCPS more time to ponder Mr. Bell's new requests for accommodation and give PCPS more time to consider and provide reasonable accommodation for Mr. Bell."

"Thank you and I appreciate your ongoing communication in efforts to accommodate Mr. Bell."

Shelly, NEA Lawyer: "I will share that information with Xander. Do you have any idea when he will be expected to report?"

"I have to correct one statement of yours below: there have been no 'new requests for accommodation.' In none of my communications with you, this week have I identified a single accommodation that was not requested months and even years ago. I appreciate yours and (district lawyer) continuing efforts in this case, but I expect it is important to be clear about what is and is not being asked."

"Thanks and have a good weekend."

District Lawyer: "I do not have a report date from HR. The goal, however, continues to be providing reasonable accommodation for Mr. Bell."

"I had not seen before the request for a scribe and/or to record meetings with administration. I will keep you posted on the report date and look forward to working with you on the matter."

"Thanks and hope you have a good weekend."

THE END OF THE CORRESPONDENCE ABOUT THE MEDIATION

By December, everything was reasonably quiet. However, they told me of some changes before the start of the new year. The Michigan Department of Civil Rights finally assigned an investigator for my case. We'll call him Peter. Shelly, my NEA lawyer, got a call from him explaining who he was and what he was doing. Shelly emailed me the info. I told her I had spoken with him. Peter would be the point man in my case now. I likewise learned that Shelly closed her time with me. They assigned Shelly to me to help with my firing but, since my status had changed, so was her work assignment. I wanted her to stay on because I had been looking to sue the school district but; I understood why she left; I just wasn't happy about it. Maybe you just get used to special people when terrible things happen, like my original NEA rep before she moved. Change is hard and having to find people to replace others is difficult.

PEEKING UNDER THE TENT: Ms. A. Juggler

Among all the cast of characters in this sad tale, Ms. Juggler has to be the one that really hit me hard. She worked with me at J. Austen HS before she made the move to Central Office. Everyone in the department determined that was great because she may pull us in for any changes we considered needed adjusting. So, when the mock EEOC test blew up in the district's face, Ms. Juggler, Mr. Popcorn and myself went right into action to fix the mistake other members of the district made. The first time she entered the classroom I realized that was odd, but I really didn't expect much of it. The second time, and times after that... literally seemed like getting stabbed in the heart. I can handle the VP and Mr. Magician, but when they pulled in Ms. Juggler; it was... personal. I was furious. I was mad at the district for pulling this stunt and I was angry at her for going along with it! When I say personal, I mean she was friends with one of my and Gaby's close acquaintances. For a while, my wife and our mutual friend stopped talking to each other. I will admit that in the meeting when I got called back for my 'great' return before we had taken our break with Ms. Juggler and Mr. Magician, I mouthed the words "I'm sorry." to Ms. Juggler. Then I immediately wished I hadn't done that. I guess the reason I did it was to see what her reaction would be. I mean, what the hell do I have to be 'sorry' about? The apology should have come from her! You know what? She put her hand up and gently nodded her head in a yes motion. What did that mean? I honestly can't read any of that. That was the last time we ever spoke again. I really wish I learned what she was pondering. I needed to identify who all influenced her. I wanted to find out... was she even sorry? Did she look humiliated or angry when they asked her to come and trash my reputation as a teacher? This one hurt the most. I guess I should be glad they didn't pull in Mr. Popcorn as well! I still have mixed emotions about this person.

Happy New Year! We've moved to January 2011. So the district wants to negotiate through a meditation about my complaint with the Human Rights people. The small problem is I don't have any legal counsel, so I emailed Kenny, my NEA rep, and like a real trooper, he gives me great news. An attorney who got recommended shared the same office as Kenny; we'll call him Cello. Crazy enough, my mediation with the school district doesn't happen for a good four months.

On Tues. April 12th, I reported to Cello's office for the pre-meeting and we talked about the general handling, what things I'd accept, and what the game-breakers were. So on the next day, Wednesday, April 13th on the 9th floor of the city hall at 10:00 am, we had our mediation event. The Human Rights organizers separated us into two different rooms before they brought us together. Dr. Clown and the school district attorney and myself and Cello introduced each other. They told us how the whole process would take place. Basically, the Human Rights people would have started with an offer from both camps and then they would share the information back and forth until we would reach some agreement. We first tried to see if the district will place me at GR. Ford HS but, I realized that was a shot in a million - they declined. The school district had literally not only offered the same plan, but they even threw in me starting on a PGP right away! Half of the time, we were trying to have them throw out the PGP. As the 11th hour was upon us - Cello, the NEA lawyer, and I had decided that just getting out of the contract with the district might be the best thing to do since they didn't show to want to do anything different.

Some time at around 6:00 pm, the Puzzle City school district finally changed the plan to where they would not start me with a PGP. They then would reserve the right to put me on a NOD immediately if I screwed up at all during this current school year so the teeth were coming out. We were getting nowhere with the district and I could tell the moderator was getting considerably irritated with the school district's behavior. I really believe the Human Right people were understanding all the nonsense of the school district. I believe there were several discussions with my lawyer Cello and the district after the epic fails of mediation. On Friday, April 15th was the finality of the end. Operation *'**get rid of the weirdo**'* was finally over. I, at least, walked away with slightly more than what they originally offered. I would resign, receive a special payment from the school district (which was infinity small compared to what I might have gotten if I had sued the Puzzle City school district), and my insurance paid for until the end of the year. Now mind you, I really concluded I would have no issue finding that new teaching job before the start of the new school year in August 2011. It will be I will spell out for you the full agreement. This is important because it will play a vital role later in my story. I just want to apologize for the legal jargon you'll be reading through:

GENERAL RELEASE AND WAIVER OF CLAIMS

COMES NOW Xander A. Bell ("Mr. Bell") and hereby executes this General Release and Waiver of Claims (the "Release"), resolving any and all claims which may exist as relates to Mr. Bell's employment with the School District of Puzzle City 69, a/k/a Puzzle City Public Schools ("PCPS").

1. Release of Claims. In consideration of PCPS's actions set forth in paragraphs 2 below, the receipt and sufficiency of which is hereby acknowledged, Mr. Bell agrees to waive, release and discharge PCPS, and all of its insurers, directors, officers, fiduciaries, employees, agents, attorneys, successors, assignors, corporations, subsidiaries, and all other entities affiliated with or related to it, without limitation, exception or reservation, from any and all liability, actions, claims, grievances, demands, or lawsuits which Mr. Bell may have had, or presently has, in connection with or arising out of his employment with PCPS. In addition:

a. Without limitation, this release applies to any and all claims, known or unknown,

arising under contract, federal, state or local statutory or common (including civil tort) law, which have been asserted or which could have been asserted, including, but not limited to, 42 U.S.C. * 1983, Title VII of the Civil Rights Act of 1964 (as amended), the Civil Rights Act of 1991, 42 U.S.C. * 1981, the Age Discrimination in Employment Act, the

Americans with Disabilities Act, the Generic Information Nondiscrimination Act of 2008, the Rehabilitation Act, the Michigan Civil Rights Act, the Family and Medical Leave Act, the Equal Pay Act, the Occupational Safety and Health Act, the Employee Retirement Income Security Act ("ERISA"), the Michigan Administrative Procedures Act (Mi. Rev. State.), the Michigan Teacher Tenure Act (Mi. Rev. Stat.), and any and all other claims under the U.S. Constitution, the Michigan Constitution, and any other federal, state, or local laws, to the maximum extent permitted by law, without limitation or exception; and

b. Without limitation, Mr. Bell also specifically and forever waives, releases and discharges any and all administrative claims or charges of discrimination, harassment, retaliation, or any other potential causes of action, including but not limited to the claims or charges that he has or has planned to file with the Equal Employment Opportunity Commission ("EEOC") and/or the Michigan Department on Civil Rights ("MDCR") and/or the Puzzle City Civil Relations Department ("PCCRD"), as well as any complaints filed or that might be filed with the U.S. Department of Education and Office of Civil Rights, along with any other such matters which Mr. Bell has filed or can have filed as of the Effective Date of this Release. Specifically, Mr. Bell agrees to withdraw his charges of discrimination, Charge Nos. E01/14-12113; 50B-2010-01959B within fifteen (15) calendar days of the execution of this Release and agrees to file all necessary documentation, with copies to PCPS, to effectuate dismissal of any and all administratively filed charges of discrimination against PCPS and/or its employees.

2. Voluntary retirement and/or resignation. In further consideration of Mr. Bell's execution of this Release, along with other good and valuable consideration set forth below, the sufficiency of which is acknowledged, upon the Effective Date of this Release, Puzzle City Public School agrees to designate Mr. Bell as having voluntarily resigned effective Thursday, June 30, 2011, and **no negative or derogatory documentation will be created and/or filed in Mr. Bell's personnel file**, other than what may already exist therein. Mr. Bell shall submit a Letter of Resignation stating that his resignation shall be effective the close of business on June 30, 2011. The Letter of Resignation shall be submitted to the Chief Legal Counsel for PCPS prior to the Effective Date of this Release. Mr. Bell shall remain an employee and shall be paid his full salary and benefits through June 30, 2011, at which time the retirement of Mr. Bell shall be effective. After June 30, 2011, Mr. Bell shall be paid for all accrued personal time off pay and sick pay accrued through June 30, 2011. Mr. Bell acknowledges and agrees that there are limits to the days and/or hours of accrued but unused personal time and sick pay to which an employee can or shall be reimbursed. Mr. Bell shall be paid only those days or hours to which he or any other employee of PCPS is or would be entitled upon

separation from employment with PCPS. Mr. Bell shall be paid a lump sum amount of $13,013 (Not the actual amount but, not far off) within fifteen (15) business days of the "Effective Date" of this Release. Mr. Bell shall be liable for any tax liability arising out of the lump sum payment and PCPS shall issue the tax form 1099 regarding such lump sum payment to Mr. Bell. Further, Mr. Bell shall be paid for reimbursement of his health insurance COBRA payment from July 1, 2011, through December 31, 2011. Mr. Bell acknowledges and agrees that this is the only outstanding consideration and/or reimbursement and no further amounts shall be paid to his for reimbursements and/or as additional consideration. All inquiries from prospective employers shall be directed to the Director of Human Resources for PCPS. In response to all inquiries from prospective employers, PCPS will provide prospective employers with a standard reply of dates of service, positions held and salary history.

3. Waiver of Existing Rights, Claims and Remedies. Mr. Bell also freely, knowingly and voluntarily waives the right to present claims and pursue other potentially applicable legal remedies, and he waives these rights, claims and/or remedies in exchange for the valuable consideration described in this Release. Mr. Bell understands that he does not waive any rights or claims that might properly arise after the date of this Release. Mr. Bell acknowledges that this Release was made available to his, through his attorney, on April 13, 2011. Mr. Bell has twenty-one

(21) calendar days after the date he received this Release to consider the Release, although he may return it sooner if desired. Mr. Bell and PCPS agree that negotiated changes to this Release (if any) before it is signed, whether material or immaterial, will not restart the twenty-one (21) day calendar day consideration period. Mr. Bell may revoke his signature to the Release after signing by delivering a written notice of revocation (by hand or by certified mail, return receipt requested) to the Puzzle City Public Schools, c/o Chief Legal Counsel, within seven (7) calendar days after he signs the Release. Mr. Bell understands that the Release will become effective and enforceable on the eighth (8th) day following the date he signs the Release (the "Effective Date").

4. No Reapplication. Mr. Bell agrees to never reapply for any position of employment with PCPS, and acknowledges this Release constitutes adequate grounds for PCPS to refuse to hire him. If Mr. Bell is somehow reemployed by PCPS, PCPS may immediately terminate his employment as a violation of this Release, with or without cause, and Mr. Bell acknowledges and understands that he has no recourse to contest such a termination. *[WHY THE HELL WOULD I WANT TO?!!!]*

5. Cooperation in Legal Proceedings. Mr. Bell agrees that he shall fully cooperate with PCPS in defense of legal claims asserted against PCPS and other matters requiring his testimony or input and knowledge.

PCPS agrees to inform Mr. Bell of any type of complaint or litigation where he is named as an individual respondent or defendant, or where his assistance is reasonably foreseen as being necessary for the defense of PCPS.

6. Non-Disclosure of Terms of Proprietary Information. Mr. Bell acknowledges that he has held, and continues to hold, a position of trust and confidence with PCPS and that, during the course of his employment, Mr. Bell may have been or has been exposed to information that is proprietary in nature, confidential to PCPS, and not generally available which, if divulged, would be potentially damaging to PCPS and/or the subject(s) of the information. Mr. Bell agrees to keep such information in strict confidence and not to disclose such information to any person except as required by law. **If Mr. Bell is required to disclose information pursuant to a court order or <u>other</u> <u>government</u> <u>process</u>, or such necessary to comply with applicable law or defend against such claims**, Mr. Bell shall: (a) notify the Legal Services Department of PCPS promptly before any such disclosure is made; (b) take all reasonably necessary steps to defend against such process or claims at PCPS's request and expense; and (c) **permit PCPS to participate with counsel of its choice in any proceeding relating to any such court order, <u>other</u> <u>government</u> <u>process</u> or claims**. In the eve this provision by Mr. Bell, this Release shall be immediately null and void and PCPS may, in

its sole discretion, proceed with any and all legal remedies available to it.

7. Non-Disclosure of Terms of Agreement/Confidentiality. The terms of this Release and the surrounding circumstances are strictly confidential except as subject to public disclosure under the Michigan Open Meetings Act, Mi. Rev. Stat.. The parties understand and agree that all discussions, negotiations, and correspondence relating to this Release and the terms thereof (collectively "Confidential Information") are strictly confidential. Mr. Bell agrees not to disclose to anyone (other than his spouse, financial advisers, legal counsel, and accountants) any Confidential Information. If Mr. Bell discloses Confidential Information to his spouse, financial advisers, counsel or accountant, Mr. Bell will make such person aware of the confidential nature of this information. **Mr. Bell agrees not to disclose any Confidential Information unless such disclosure is: (i) <u>lawfully required by any government agency</u>; (ii)** otherwise required to be disclosed by law, and/or by court order; or (iii) necessary in any legal proceeding in order to enforce any provision of this Agreement. Mr. Bell may respond to any inquiry about the status and/or resolution of this matter by stating that the matter has been resolved by the mutual agreement of the parties and is confidential.

8. Signature, Executed, and Authorization. Mr. Bell warrants he has read completely and understands the provisions of this Release, and has executed this Release voluntarily and without duress.

9. Advice of Counsel. Mr. Bell acknowledges that he has had the opportunity to and has been encouraged to consult with legal counsel regarding the meaning and effect of this Release, including all terms and conditions and has, in fact, consulted with legal counsel regarding the same.

10. Headings. The headings of sections contained in this Release are for convenience only and shall not be deemed to control or effect a meaning or construction of any provisions of this Release.

11. Applicable Law. Mr. Bell agrees that the terms and provisions of this Release shall be interpreted and enforced under the substantive laws of the State of Michigan, to the extent state law applies, and under federal law, to the extent, federal law applies.

ACKNOWLEDGED AND AGREED TO BY XANDER BELL.

4-21-11

Xander Bell (Signed in RED ink)

This was my official letter of resignation to which I signed in red ink on purpose. I consider my signature on both documents in red says exactly of how I felt. I gave most of my teaching career to this school district. I guess you can literally say blood, sweat, and tears. So the red signature was my way of telling Puzzle City that I had given everything I had to their district and instead, get sacrificed all because our Pontius Pilate wanted me permanently gone.

Date:

April 21, 2011

Board of Education Puzzle City Public Schools 1959 Allen Road, Puzzle City, Michigan 49034

Dear Members of the Board of Education:

I hereby submit my irrevocable letter of resignation from the Puzzle City Public Schools effective June 30, 2011. I am resigning for personal reasons.

Sincerely,

Xander Bell (Again, signed in RED ink)

As the dust has settled, I received an official letter from the Human Relations Department, which stated:

Mr. Bell;

A preliminary investigation has been completed in the case of Xander Bell v. Puzzle City Michigan School District.

As the Manager of the Civil Rights Division, Department of Human Relations, I have rendered a Determination of Withdrawal with Benefits.

We are pleased that a satisfactory settlement has been reached on the issues raised in your complaint. If you have any questions about the terms of the settlement mean or any other questions on what your rights now are, we would be happy to discuss them with you.

If the Respondent fails, in your opinion, to satisfactorily comply with the terms of the settlement, you should advise this office immediately.

If you have any questions or if, in the future, you have a situation with which we might be able to help, I hope that you will call upon the Department of Human Relations.

Sincerely,

Human Relations Department

With that, I finished my time with the High Flying Circus Show... The Puzzle City School District. In some sense, the relief of knowing that I would never have to jack with them was amazing and sad in others. I invested, roughly, 15 years of my teaching career to one place only to have it end like that, no encore, no retirement banquet, anniversary pins, awards, plaques for my service, or thank you's... just a release.

CIRCUS RING #3

(RIGHT RING)

Chapter 10: Finding A New Act

During the time I had with Kenny, my NEA rep, I had been trying to get that new teaching job. Remember, the sticking point was how I was still under contract with PCPS and I really can't sign a new contract with another school district since I was still under theirs. I had little success in getting interviews with school districts in my area. Kenny and my NEA people really made a strong push to get me interviews. From the time I split from the school district, all the way through most of the 2011-2012 school year, I tried hard to get back into a school. I will chronicle all the different schools I applied with and yes... all the different states. My first three interviews were in Missouri at the instance of my NEA rep Kenny. Sadly the towns selected other candidates but, at least the NEA helped me get interviews with these districts since my NEA rep was from the state plus I attended college in Missouri - Northwest Missouri State. I want to let you understand that I kept in mind that I was older and that might play a part since that would have made me more expensive in my salary. I remember when I was just starting out trying to find my first teaching job, the thing I kept hearing from schools that turned me down was "we're looking for someone with a little more experience." That statement unnerved me because logically, 'How was I supposed to get experience if I didn't get the chance to begin somewhere?'

The passage of time had changed for the HRs in several schools. They were now looking for candidates that were young and cheap. I honestly found that unbelievable. How twisted was our education system about teacher hiring? I had done my student teaching with the North Kansas City schools while I was at NWMS but, I never had the chance to get hired on with North Kansas City Schools, not that I didn't try hard. As I turned my attention to Kansas, I applied with schools from Shawnee Mission, Olathe, and Blue Valley. Those three districts are not that small: They have several high schools so right there you recognize the student base is large.

 My wife and I were coming into May and no sign of a job. Gaby was not too thrilled with Missouri or Kansas; maybe Michigan would have been better. Gaby and I looked way out of state and my first target was Alaska... I'm not kidding. I had heard that Alaska was always in need of teachers so Gaby and I seemed like if we had to move then that was a sacrifice we would make. The school district I applied with was in Anchorage. I judged it would be the best choice since that was the largest city. Since I started with Alaska, Gaby and I guessed well why not Colorado, Oregon or Washington - so I filled out an application with Pueblo City Schools in Colorado, Corbett schools in Corbett, Oregon and the Spokane school district in Washington State. I'm sure you're speculating, 'Why not my home state of Michigan?' honestly, I was tired of Michigan and Gaby and I wanted to move. Puzzle City was good, but we needed a real change.

By this point, the ball started rolling fast. There was no limit to where I applied in the United States. I hopped back to Colorado and applied with the Weld School district in Keenesburg, CO, Harrison schools in Colorado Springs, CO, another school in Pueblo called Chavez-Huerta (not once but twice!). I zipped back to Oregon to the Molalla River school district in Molalla, OR, Oakland schools in Oakland, OR, Reynolds Schools in Fairview, OR, Lincoln County Schools in Newport, OR, Tigard-Tualatin Schools in Tigard, OR, Salem-Keizer schools in Salem, OR and Port Orford-Langlois School District in Port Orford, OR.

 I can't pass up a chance to apply for a teaching position and department chair in Pekin Community Schools in Pekin, Illinois. (At least it was slightly closer to Michigan) I guessed it was long odds but, I will try everything. I realize as you read this you are questioning why the heck am I naming every school district I applied with, the best answer I can give you at this point is I wanted you to see how desperate I was in getting that next teaching position and how the Puzzle City Public School might play into this.

I assumed I'd reach out to another state Minnesota, and the school was Mankato Area Public Schools in Mankato, MN, Albany public schools in Albany, MN, the Buffalo-Hanover-Montrose schools in Buffalo, MN, Roseville Schools in Roseville, MN and the Bemidji School District in Bemidji, MN. My intention for applying with these different schools in different states was that I tried to imagine what the area would look like and the school building itself. I really attacked this new employment strategy. I tried Smithville High School and Marshall Public Schools. I'm mid-June now and I still had my foot on the gas pedal. I revisited Pueblo City, CO to apply for three more teaching jobs they had an opening, Swink School District in Swink, CO.

I applied with the Bellevue School District in Bellevue, Washington, and the Tacoma School District in Tacoma, Washington. I even applied for a position as a History/Bible Teacher at the Portland Christian School in Portland, OR, I filled out an application with Glendale School District in Glendale, OR, Roseburg Schools in Roseburg, Oregon, Ontario Schools in Ontario, OR, Klamath Falls Schools in Klamath Falls, OR, Bend-La Pine Schools in Bend, OR, Three Rivers Schools in Murphy, OR and I applied with Bandon Schools in Bandon, OR.

I figured it was about time to look at the state that houses the second-largest city in America...California. I applied with San Jose Unified in San Jose, CA, Hacienda La Puente Unified in Industry, CA, Coalinga-Huron Unified in Coalinga, CA, Cutler-Orosi Unified in Orosi, CA, Redondo Beach Unified in Redondo Beach, CA, Newark Unified in Newark, CA. I wasn't so sure about Los Angeles, but I filled out an application with Cabrillo Unified in Half-Moon Bay, CA, Morgan Hill Unified in Morgan Hill, CA, San Juan Unified in Carmichael, CA, Leadership Public Schools in San Jose, CA (which I found out are now closed for good), another school in San Jose - Escuela Popular and Ukiah Unified in Ukiah, CA.

I really wanted to apply in Michigan but, Gaby just told me no and not even Indiana which surprised me. I needed to share just how determined I was. I'm sure you're expecting I'm making the most of this stuff up...the only reason I remembered these places is because I kept every email that sends me a confirmation of my application with these school districts. I would sometimes receive rejection letters through email so let me take a minute to share one:

Dear Mr. Bell,

Thank you for taking the time to apply and express your interest in the Social Studies Teacher position at Phoenix Charter School in Roseburg, Oregon. We've carefully reviewed your qualifications; however, we have pursued other candidates with skills and experience that more closely match the needs of the school.

We will keep your application on file until the close of the search if our employment needs change. Again, thank you for your interest in Phoenix Charter School.

Best,

Phoenix Charter Schools HR

I guess the sentence that really threw me off was "...
we have pursued other candidates with skills and
experience that more closely matched the needs of
the school." Really?!!! Nearly two decades of teaching
and got groomed by a major university to be an
adjunct professor to teach college World History?
That experience?!!! It was letters like these that I
honestly can't believe that they were literally saying
these things to me.

I still had to "keep on, keeping on," so I tried Twin
Falls City School in Twin Falls City, Idaho, Cassia
County Schools in Burley, Idaho; The Native
American and Youth Family Center in Portland,
Oregon (I have a family history of the Choctaw Tribe,
sadly my Great-Great grandmother did not register
so there were no papers on her.), I applied with El
Reno Public Schools in El Reno, Oklahoma, and really
why not? Many of my relatives either live or have
lived in Oklahoma so it made sense...especially
considering Oklahoma has had an issue with a
teacher shortage. I further tried Woodward Public
Schools in Woodward, Oklahoma. I guessed I'd try a
school district that my principal used to be an
administrator with and that was the Yuma High
School District in Yuma, Arizona. Dr. R. Strongman
wrote this in an email to me:

Hi Xander,

I just completed a reference for you for Yuma. Let me know if you hear or get an interview. I've worked with most of the administrators down there from my time as a principal with the elementary district. I can make a call on your behalf.

Good Luck!

(Dr. E. Strongman)

The email made me feel fantastic, and I knew I'd have a great chance of getting on the Yuma School District. I was trying so hard and I was looking outside the box at positions that I really wasn't sure if I was qualified for, though I found out that most of them I was.

August slid in and then September. I had several interviews but no takers by this point. My NEA rep really wanted me to give Missouri and Kansas one more try, but my luck in those states didn't bode well. Kenny wasn't going to let this go so I gave it one more chance applying for Liberty Schools, and Kansas City, KS again. In November, I tried Blue Springs and Olathe again. After the applications were finished, I finally told Kenny to just forget it. I know he was only doing his job, but Gaby and I decided to stay in Michigan.

So in the course of 2011, I had applied with lots of schools in... yes...12 different states. {Alaska, Arizona, California, Colorado, Idaho, Illinois, Kansas, Minnesota, Missouri, Oklahoma, Oregon, Washington} I did not receive one... single... job offer from any... school I just listed. I'm sorry you had to pour through all of those schools but, I expect I made my point explicitly clear on how badly I was trying to get a new teaching position. During the time of my job search, I started questioning a tiny sample size of schools to see if they had heard anything from my former employer. Those few I asked told me they had heard nothing... but I had made a mistake. I asked the principals when I really should have been inquiring with Human Resources.

My teacher's instinct let me recognize that school was about to start, but without me involved. I had turned to Vocational Rehabilitation to help me with my eyes now being set on the business sector. I learned that my resume needed work. Her name was Mary (not the real name) and she worked with a firm to help people like me. The problem with Voc. Rehab. that since I was a highly educated professional, it would be difficult for them to help me. In all honesty, Mary was about the only person I needed. I was finding myself wanting to stay in my office/craft room where the family computer sat. Settling there, I can fill out job applications online or do other things I wanted with no one around to bother me. I will admit that my psychiatrist ordered me to get out of the office and interact with the family more. That assignment was difficult since I didn't see any purpose or benefit. I didn't consider myself to be a real husband or father without having a job. I had the one responsibility that I had as the husband and that was one who financed the family. My wife had stayed home to raise the children while I worked, and now I can't even do that.

One thing I had to face during my time trying to find a job was depression. I sensed the dark atmosphere beginning after all the harsh attacks on me when I was still at J. Austen HS; which created me to be more fearful and terrified. You could say I was borderline PTSD (Post Traumatic Stress Disorder). Once I finally left, I hoped my mood had changed for the better, but I realized I'd only been fooling myself. The problem with depression, at least I found, is you don't realize you have it. Since I'm a creature of habit and will do roughly the same thing every day, my awareness of my state of depression didn't seem to hit me. I've learned that depression has a way of drifting and methodically consuming you to where it gradually sinks in and you're unaware of it.

The difficult part involved Gaby, not only was I during this debilitating emotion but my wife was going through the motions, and I believe even worse than I was. The day would usually start with breakfast and then I would go into our study and get on the computer while Gaby stayed in her bed and watched movies. I was busy filling out job applications online, but getting out and being active was foreign to me. Sometimes I just played on the computer, but I made a real effort in trying to gain employment. I remember my wife trying to encourage me to get up and do something, but my comfort was better suited in the office.

When I started applying with businesses, there were new things I had to learn when I interviewed with any company. Insurance was one of the biggest factors in any decision on whether I would accept a job proposal. The other was earnings because I was earning slightly over 50K a year and I was hoping to find something around the same salary. Strangely, my first inquiry was from an email I received from Olandlab from the country of Sweden. I did some digging with the company and they sounded fine, so I emailed my information, but I didn't hear from the company after my initial letter. The second place I applied with WireCo which sounded interesting, but nothing really came from that job. My first real job application and the interview were with Ferrellgas. I considered the interview sounded odd as it only lasted for about 10 minutes, but that's how it led. Since I made the move to 'on the other side of the fence' applications, interviews, and other unknown things were now coming into play. I was learning as I moved. I had a salary and benefits, but the biggest trick was to figure out how my teaching qualification and college education might play a part in a full-blown company. My aim was to look more at training positions or possibly Human Resources, but I figured that might be a stretch.

I applied with a company called IXL Learning as a History Curriculum Designer just to give you an idea of what I was finding. There were other companies that I honestly had no idea what they did or what the name was because I was getting desperate; a great example was NAIC or WIS International. I wasn't sure who they were but; the job was one I knew I can do. I filled out an application for a training position with Sungevity, Alliance Data, BNSF Railways, Waddell & Reed, and Lexmark. Since I had a Bachelor's in Communication, I hoped I'd use that to my advantage. I applied with Houghton Mifflin Harcourt Publishing in trusting they might select me because working for a publishing company was appealing to me. I found educational opportunities in hospitals, and one I remember applying with a few occasions was the Children's Hospital of Michigan. Another job I tried with education behind it was at PNC Savings Bank where I filled out an application for a Learning and Development Specialist and H and R Block as a Training Developer. I tried LinkedIn, a popular social media website for professionals. I believe LinkedIn is an excellent site to check out.

I would constantly check in with Mary who had been trying hard to find me any job leads. Mary did a great job of helping me out. I applied with Sprint, VinSolutions as Virtual Trainer, Brookdale as a Sales

Training Specialist just to name a few. Let me share with you a series of emails between Mary and myself to give you a good idea of what I've done and her reaction:

October 14, 2011

Mary,

Here is the list:

WireCo - Pricing Specialist; Alliance Data (2) - Trainer / Leadership Dev. Program; Lexmark - Edu. Service Trainer; Cerner - Senior Learning Consul; PNC - Learning Dev. Specialist; Waddell & Reed - Training Specialist; Giarmarco, Mullins, and Horton - Brand Planner; MacFarlane Group - Corporate Trainer; Smithfield - Talent Dev. Man; Spencer/Reed Group (2) - Coord. Education / Coord-Admin Asst; Cengage Learning-Educational Sales Consult; Houghton Mifflin Harcourt - Per Diem Literacy Consul; Sprint - Sales Project-Program Manager III; Shook Hardy Bacon - Practice Manager; Oracle (3) - Product Training Man / Dir, Ed. Industry Solution / Course-Curriculum Dev.3- Training; Dairy Farmers of America - Publication Manager; Ascend Learning - Executive Dir; Experis - Instructional Designer; ICONMA - E-Learning Dev; Anthony Adams - E-Learning Dev; HigherEchelon - E- Learning Dev; Ferrellgas - Corporate Trainer-Inst.

Designer; K-Force - Recruiter; ZeroChaos - Corporate Recruiter; Aba - Dir of Digital Ed.and Online Learning; Outback - Regional Trainer; CEVA - Operations Super; Favorite HealthCare Staffing - Quality Assurance Coord; ProLogistix - Transportation Coord; SPX - HR Generalist; SwoonTech - Training Coord; Vitalograph Inc. - Project Manager; Merlin Ent.(Legoland) (2) - Marketing Man / Commercial Super; UM MedCenter - Recruiter; FedEx - Field HR Specialist; EPCOR - Dir. of ACH Rules and Ed; Kalamazoo College - Dir. of Undergrad; HR-Heaven - Human Resources Generalist; Michigan NonProfit Association - Dir. of E-Learning.

That's the list so far!

Xander

October 15, 2011

Xander,

Would it be possible for you to add contact information so I can follow up with the person who received your information?

Thanks.

Mary

Also, didn't you apply to United Health Group?

October 15, 2011

Mary,

That might take some time because I'm not sure about several of these jobs and who the contact person is. I have Tom S. who was the main person for Ferrellgas. I must get the rest. I applied with the United Health Group, but I got a Dear John letter yesterday when I was meeting with you.

Xander

I emailed several follow-ups yesterday, and I applied for two more jobs: Shook Hardy Bacon - Trainer and TBC Corporation - Sales Trainer Supervisor.

And really, I could continue on for quite some time on all the businesses I had applied for, but I'll just narrow it down. The three significant jobs they offered me was a salesperson for Time Warner Cable, a display organizer for Home Depot and assistant manager at Walgreens. I didn't take the sales position because they would have based my salary on the number of sales and honestly, I never thought I'd be a good salesman. I didn't accept the display organizer or the assistant manager for one reason... insurance. I was getting closer to the end of the year and my health insurance was about to run out. I don't blame these corporations by putting a delay on new employees before gaining health insurance. Sadly, I didn't have the time. I needed a job where my insurance would start at the same time my job did. As the year 2011 was ending, hopes for a job seemed to dwindle.

My situation at the end of the year was probably the most difficult my wife and I had to deal with, with my trying to find a new job and the lack of finances we were beginning to experience. We looked to food stamps and any other assistance we could find, including our utilities. I will always be grateful to our family who set up and helped us when we needed it the most. In October, Gaby and I faced a new financial crisis where our mortgage company was ready to take our house right behind our backs. Gaby was smart enough to get a hold of the people at Legal Aid and they advised us to immediately go to our Federal Courthouse and file for Chapter 13 bankruptcy to save the house from being auditioned. I can say that was probably the biggest battle we had that year against our own mortgage company! I believe if it wasn't for our faith and family, we would never have made it through the severe financial windfall we experienced that year.

 From my journal during the week of December 25th and January 1st, this is what I observed: "Having the whole family at my parent's house for Christmas was great, but it still didn't sound the same. I'm getting desperate because the money is about gone and I still have no job. I have to give (my problems) to the Lord. I really can't write much because I am overwhelmed.

This will take a true miracle from the Lord for my family to be yanked out from this darkness. So ends the year of 2011. I can only pray for the Lord to guide us in the New Year... As of 2012, I now have no health insurance and still no job. I still believe God has a plan, but we really need his help immediately!"

Chapter 11: The Whole Plot Is Exposed

There was one particular event that happened to me in the early part of 2012. This involves an organization that worked alongside the unemployment department of Michigan called The Michigan Works! or TMW for short. The description of their organization comes from its own website:

"TMW is a business-led private non-profit corporation whose mission is to obtain public and private sector employment for the unemployed and underemployed residents of the Greater Puzzle City area. TMW accomplishes this goal by working in collaboration with businesses, local units of government, educational institutions, labor, and community-based organizations. This partnership responds to employer needs while reducing unemployment, underemployment, and the public dependency of area residents. The TMW supplies employers with a skilled workforce by getting public and private sector employment for the unemployed and underemployed residents of Hilldale, Jackson, Lenawee, and Washtenaw County."

Now, as you just read, it set this up for the Puzzle City Metro Area. I'm not sure how other cities and states work their system but, I learned if you search for your state's unemployment program, I'm sure there will be some good information to help get you started. For a while, the TMW helped me in my search for a job and they even had a 'job club' that I attended so I received a suggestion that maybe I should apply with the TMW themselves. The job I applied for was a Career Coach, but the official title was Career Development Executive. I was qualified. Like I said earlier, see how far you can stretch your abilities. So I had my first initial interview with one of TMW's HR people. They told me that if everything sounded good, then I'd be looking at a few more interviews from higher officials. The wait for the second interview took a while, and I was wondering if I really would have a chance to move on. I got the second interview, and it was with the TMW's senior vice-president and COO. I loved the interview because she was nice and easy to talk to. The COO told me I would have one more interview, and that was with the President and CEO of TMW. When I finally met with the CEO, he looked to be eccentric, but I found him to be fascinating. The only thing that took me by surprise in the interview was the job description. When I spoke with the COO, she told me a few things she'd like to see from the job and since I was a former teacher, she saw the potential in revamping the position.

When I talked with the CEO, his vision of the position was slightly different. I remember discussing the position's duties with the COO, so I was testing to see if the two top people had even communicated with each other. The interview was good, and I didn't see any real issues. Try to understand, when I finished with the interview, I had several people within the organization inform me that if I make it all the way to the President, then the job gets guaranteed. This didn't come from one person; it came from several. Since I spent more time in and around their offices, I had noticed a few employees there.

 So now I get to set you up for the next series of events that will completely floor anyone but, all true. I hadn't heard from the TMW for about a week until I received a call one day. They told me they were trying to get a hold of the Puzzle City MI School District to verify my employment because there was no return call or FAX. This forced me to contact my NEA lawyer to have him contact the district so we might get the process started and prep me for my new job. The TMW was good enough to tell me that the school district finally communicated with them but that was it. No questions, no need to clear any issues, they just made contact. Roughly two weeks after my last contact with TMW, I receive a letter in the mail and this is what it said:

Dear Mr. Bell:

Thank you for your interest in The Michigan Works! (TMW) and for taking the time to interview for the position of Career Development Executive. Although your credentials were respectable, you did not get selected for this position.

It was a pleasure to meet with you, and we wish you the best in your future endeavors.

S.D.

Human Resources

Surprised? I sure was! There was only one thing I could do. I called the person who sent me the letter. The only thing she would tell me was I needed to be careful whom I assumed I could trust as a source. I didn't get any details and so they left me wondering who was behind this confusion. So I guess you can say the place that was supposed to help get me a job couldn't give me a job!!! Suddenly, an ominous thought came over me. During the time I waited for this letter, I had wondered if Dr. M. Clown had left PCPS? Understand that when we last talked, Dr. Clown had mentioned that she was heading back to Ann Arbor, MI where she's from and be a part of the University there. I did some digging into the PCPS website and under the HR department, Dr. Clown wasn't there, but no head of HR got listed on the page. I realized that was weird because the district always made it known who the point person was for the head of HR. I had to do some serious searching, but I finally found that, in fact, she was still running the Human Resources department! My disappointment of not getting the job with the TMW was still fresh but, by far, this was my first real 'red flag' about the school district. This was only speculation at first, but I now had more tangible evidence that my old employer was up to no good.

In April 2012, I attended a job fair at a college that both my wife and I attended, Michigan University. [I attended for my Master's; the Bachelors were from Northwest Missouri State] When I was there; I met two different federal government agencies in attendance. I didn't say too much about them but it will play a much bigger role than I ever dreamed possible later that year. Later in May, I met up with a contracting company that worked alongside the federal government. During the time, I was doing the background checks and fingerprinting, I was still applying with federal government jobs. Sadly, the government job didn't work out so I did the next best thing... I finally got hired by the contracting company called DLF Federal.

This company worked alongside the USCIS or United States Citizenship and Immigration Services. The department falls under the umbrella of the Department of Homeland Security. My official start date was June 20, 2012, and the job was General Clerk... that wasn't a typo. This man of over 20 years of teaching experience, with a Bachelor's and Master's Degree, gets relegated to a clerk... with my starting salary at $12.95 an hour. Was it humiliating? Yes. I was a trained professional in education. I viewed this experience as a serious blow. I realize, however, that I kind of needed a reality check. I already realize what you're guessing. "What the hell was I expecting?" Well... as I stated earlier, I received other job offers but, not one job allowed me to have my health insurance start day one. Since my insurance expired as of December 31, 2012, I was definitely on the clock. DLF Federal was the only job offer I received that was: one, full time, and two, the insurance starts immediately. I was still seeking federal jobs, but at least I was now on the inside!

I have to admit that the job was considerably interesting, DLF is a leading provider of enduring support for the essential missions of the U.S. government, its allied partners and international organizations. With over 60 years of experience, DLF supports the execution of complex and critical missions by providing global logistics and stability operations, technical services and national security solutions to customers around the world. In this role, you will support the customer mission by processing applications for individuals on their path to citizenship. General Clerks are responsible for reviewing files and identifying all names and DOB variations related to that individual. The resulting information is then entered into a computer database. This position requires the ability to sit and read pages of information for long periods of time. Strong attention to detail, data entry, and keyboarding accuracy and proficiency are critical to the role. During my time there, I had the chance to change my duties, and I moved to the file room and got the delivery and audit files. I really liked the work that I did, but that's not the most revealing part of this story. Every single person who gets hired to either work as a contractor or an actual employee of the government is thoroughly.... and I mean THOROUGHLY, checked and interviewed by the Office of Personnel Management. I need to take a minute to give complete details on the OPM or Office of Personnel Management. What they do I pulled directly from their website, it states:

"The U.S. Office of Personnel Management (OPM) serves as the chief human resource agency and personnel policy managers for the Federal Government. OPM provides human resources leadership and support to Federal agencies and helps the Federal workforce achieve their aspirations as they serve the American people. OPM directs human resources and employee management services, administers retirement benefits, manages healthcare and insurance programs, oversees merit-based and inclusive hiring into the civil services, and provides a secure employment process."

I'm sure you're speculating, 'big deal, what does that have to do with our problem?' The thing is you are being questioned by the United States government where OPM has all intelligence about you at their fingertips. My bosses advised me to be honest. Not one lie about anything because they will know... somehow, someway, they will always know. When I got hired, the OPM interview didn't happen right away. Usually, there is a grace period and they need the time to gather the information... your information. These folks do not play around. Each person is a licensed and badge-carrying (literally) inspector or better... an adjudicator.

Now that you understand what they do, when I started the job back in June, I learned interviews would take place I just wasn't sure when. Some of my colleagues started getting their interviews and at one point, I was assuming they would skip me since I had been a teacher in the past. To be a teacher, we all had to go through background checks for children's safety. Well... I was wrong. My interview finally came on November 5, 2012. The agent was nice, though I admitted I was slightly nervous. She showed me her badge to prove she was legit and thumbed through her notes. The agent started off with the usual simple questions like name, family, address, schooling. She asked me about my health history and my autism diagnosis. Then the discussion turned to my places of employment. She asked about my first school district (Three Rivers, MI), the second school district (Cold Water, MI), and my final school district PCPS. The agent wanted more details about my time there. She wanted to identify my job description, the layoff in 2005, and what happened at the conclusion of my job.

Even though I realized they restricted me from giving any details on the harassment charges, there was one exception and it was about the government, under

Article #7 of my agreement, in part. This is what it stated: "Mr. Bell agrees not to disclose any Confidential Information unless such disclosure is: (i) lawfully required by any government agency..." and guess who's asking... OPM. I became legally bound to tell the agent everything. And I did without hesitation.

Then something weird happened... I remember her telling me, "Oh, okay... that might explain things." I didn't understand what she meant by "things". All I could pull together was that it was important. So the agent took out a manila envelope and removed one sheet of paper. She told me that this was new information they had received from PCPS and she wanted to read it to me. The agent first stated the dates they had employed me with the district. Then she read that I was "not eligible for rehire" which made sense with the cutting of the tides.

And then there was one.... more.... thing the agent directly said: "that the Puzzle City Public Schools stated that I was... **unfavorable for employment**."

Like a crack of thunder exploding in my head, every single memory I had about all of those school applications and missed interviews came rushing in all at once. I finally got the answer to my longing question. The very thing that the HR department was trying to conceal. The jolt of the news completely threw me off so much the first thing I uttered was, "What did you say?"

I expected the agent had to be lying to me. I'm sure my clarifying question surprised the agent. I would only assume she thought I didn't completely understand, so the agent was nice enough to restate the quote, "meaning" she emphasized, "**you're unemployable**."

The revision of her adjusted definition didn't make the message any better. The quote just sunk a lot harder in my chest. The rush of blood emptied from my head and I almost collapsed. To say it enraged me... really didn't give the full picture.

I have to admit that after my meeting, I was in a fog. My condition was so bad even the agent had to ask if I was all right? With my Asperger's brain, I realized this information would take some time to disseminate. I remember leaving the meeting reflecting all the unexplained lost opportunities with school districts and the way The Michigan Works! treated me. They're just sometimes you wish that people would stick to their word, or better yet, their written agreement. I called my NEA lawyer next and told him about the revelation. He told me I could contact a defamation lawyer, but this would be a case that was out of his practice. So with the stroke of information that got delivered to me by the Federal Government, my agreement with the Puzzle City Public School became null and void! For me, I had mixed emotions where I finally got vindication but I was still outraged. I always had a hard time trusting most of the people in the front office and, when you finally have the evidence that proves you were right, it doesn't make my revelation feel any better.

Ironically, later that year I got selected by the USCIS for a government job as an Office Automation Assistant and you recognize what that meant... yup, another OPM interview. The only distinction was I would be even more thoroughly investigated because I was seeking a higher security clearance. This meant that they would interview my bosses, my family, and my neighbors. Yes, that really happened. The special agent I worked with was nice. The only variation between the two was that the second one wanted me to hand over all the information I had about the discrimination case. She wanted to review the information to make a ruling. After she finished the investigation, I remembered her telling me I should really seek a lawyer. After sadly Obama had to put a stop on all government hiring... including me. My time to be employed with the government was dwindling fast.

However, that is not the end of my tale. Something weird and amazing happened in the summer of 2013. My wife still wanted me to get a teaching job, but I really wasn't all that thrilled because I still believed I had a real chance at being a Federal Government employee. Puzzle City INDIANA School District was holding a job fair on July 11th. Puzzle City sits on the borders of Michigan and Indiana. Gaby and I traveled down to Indiana to be interviewed for a teaching position. I interviewed for the Social Studies position and Gaby interviewed for Special Education. Gaby got offered a contract right there on the spot and I got a thank you and a handshake. I was really excited for my wife, but I was so fed up with school districts I didn't care anymore... but can you blame me? So I continued with my contractor job with the government, and Gaby was preparing to go back in the classroom. When Gaby started, something odd happened and I recorded this in my journal from the week of August 4th through 10th of 2013:

As Gaby started school on Wednesday, August 7th, people from the district started asking if the person she was with on the interview back in July was a co-teacher. She told them I was her husband and was a teacher for a long time. Puzzle City Indiana School District asked if I had an interest in working in SPED for the district. She said she wasn't sure, but would talk to me about the offer. (I literally had to contemplate about it.) I decided I would give teaching another try. The only real reason I moved back was that I identified the job would be different this time. Special Education is what I chose and it will be different. On Saturday, August 10th, Puzzle City Indiana had another job fair, and I sat in with a small presentation first, then the interviews. (Gaby was with me only because several people told her that "They would see her Saturday.")

She had no real reason to be there, but I understand it was for curiosity and emotional support. I sat down on three separate interviews: one person from BJ Harrison High School, the second was two women from Bronte Middle School, (the school that Gaby teaches at) they wanted to understand how I would behave working with my wife. The third was interesting — the lady who supervised the high schools didn't have any paper for notes; she was direct and straight to the point. They offered me a SPED position at E.V. Debs High School, and so despite all the bull crap I had put up with from PCPS... I accepted the offer to teach again, this time in Indiana.

Don't give up. So easy to say but hard to engage. Having to deal with my lost job, my retirement and overall income has been a huge hit to my family, but I believe we'll survive. Going through these series of events can pull us down. But, even if you may not have gotten diagnosed with autism, job harassment is a real problem. I like to assume the reason we're working is that we are trying to provide for ourselves and/or our family. You should never have to work in silence if either co-workers or even your boss is harassing you because you might be slightly different on the outside or — like me — on the inside. Never accept the conditions of how things go at your work! Your job should never be a place you're afraid to work just because of inhumane supervisors or colleagues.

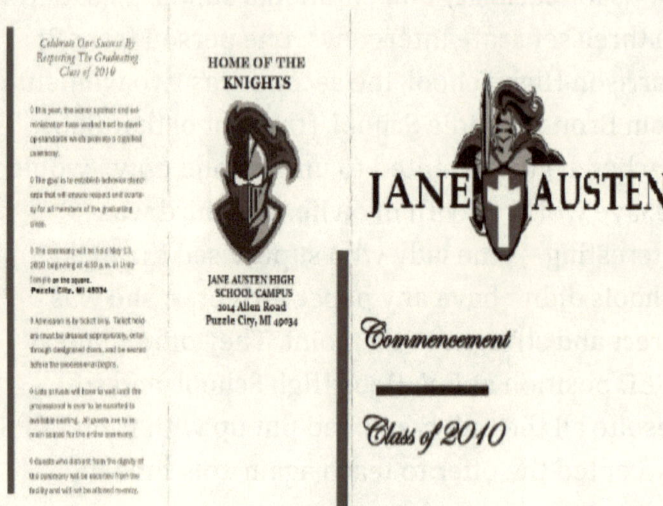

Even though I didn't get the chance to attend the graduation, I still at least got a program!

CIRCUS RING #4

(THE SIDESHOW)

Chapter 12: Stand Up and Move Ahead

I'm sure you now understand the condition I faced when I worked for the Puzzle City School District. I've read several success stories about all kinds of people with Autism Spectrum Disorder breaking barriers and gaining careers that we may only have dreamed of doing. I'm thrilled to hear about these stories. My main concern is keeping them! Employers need to understand how to handle people like us and what the best course of action would be rather than just firing them... or humiliate them first, then terminate them. I have sadly heard too many stories of people with ASD who were teased, bullied, and dehumanized before they were fired. And as you read in my story, the Silent Discrimination affected me in a big way.

Having the condition of High Functioning Autism not only makes the job difficult, but the personal life can also take a hit as well. We seek friendship, but we can get frustrated if there isn't a true understanding of our condition. Therefore, marriage can be very difficult to manage. In conversation, a couple will talk about different things and have an interest. The thing is that each person needs to listen to each other and engage in the discussion together. My problem is knowing when enough is enough and shut up... one in which my wife completely agrees with! Sometimes, our fine motor skills might be off so this makes us look like we're physically awkward or clumsy.

I take medication for my condition, but I will admit this came with a lot of trial and error. Some medicines either made me angry all the time or really lazy. The reason I take the medication is because of my high anxiety, depression, and obsessive-compulsive behavior, better known as OCD. When I was looking for a new job, one thing my wife Gaby and I discussed was sharing my information. When I apply for a job, do I tell the potential employer that I have Autism Spectrum Disorder? Honestly, we traveled back and forth on the subject. Sometimes I disclosed my condition and then there were other times I didn't. We really were not sure. The decision looked like a guessing game. We believe I should mention the disorder on the application. Some ASD organizations would tell people who have gotten diagnosed that accommodations aren't necessary, but I completely disagree! Every single person with this condition should have some accommodations on file with their employees to put in... you don't understand what situation might come up that would directly affect your condition. We're not fortune-tellers, we don't predict what imminent event might happen that we can foresee. Always have accommodations to cover yourself.

Sometimes I question myself on how I got through those attacks. I can't lie to you and say I never contemplated suicide, but my faith in Jesus is the main reason why I'm still here. I believe most people enjoy music, but for me this is critical. Having to make those trips to J. Austen and back was difficult, but I remember several times when I'm listening to the radio and the station plays a song that speaks about my whole life. Before I can get home, I'm crying like a baby. The songs that had a huge impact on me were Danny Gokey's "Rise", For King and Country's "Shoulders", Eminem's "Not Afraid", Superchick's "Still Here", Johnny Cash's "Hurt", POD's "Alive" and several others, but they each had their own special place. I strongly encourage you to embrace the music that speaks to you. We all go through our nightmares and they test our resolve, but it's not the end. Encouraging music does help. It helped me.

I guess looking back at those challenging times I can't help but echo on a few things. The first thing would have to be the mistakes I made and what I learned. I learned never to stand on a desk to fix a window blind. I learned I need to remember the person I'm speaking to, what I said and what is best left alone. I learned real leadership is a gift that only specific people have, and the rest are just pretending. I learned that people will do anything to keep their job no matter how severe the ethical consequences can be. I learned colleagues are not always your real friends. I learned never... never trust someone at their face value, especially some people in HR. If it weren't for those silver linings, as horrible as my experience was, I guess I won't be writing this story today. You have to break through the inferno to gain a true epiphany for the perils in life. I have to admit that deep down when I made those trips to school in my VW Rabbit, I honestly had wished I could just leave my job. I guess I thought it trapped me because I was the only main source of income and I couldn't risk giving everything up and getting a new job, especially with the salary I had already established. If this whole thing wasn't about my disability, the whole story might have ended differently. But it got personal. Reading stories of other people like me who have the same disability just broke my heart.

So here are my thoughts on one thing I wish I knew about every main personality in this book:

Dr. E. Strongman - I wished I knew what he would have done differently when he was the principal.

Mr. K. Tamer - I wished I knew if he assumed he's happier with a new job in a new school district.

Dr. J. Dollar - I wished I knew how the hell he expected merging middle school into high school would be a good idea.

Dr. S. Ringmaster - I wished I knew if he slept well at night knowing some very inhumane decisions he's made to his school personnel over the years.

Mr. T. Tightrope - I wished I knew how he could keep his job after the huge computer program screws up.

Dr. E. Fire-Eater - I wished I knew if she would ever understand how to be a true educational leader and not a terrible judge of personalities.

Ms. T. Audience - I wished I knew if she learned a valuable lesson from my meeting and her dysfunctional colleagues.

Mr. A. Big-Top - I wished I knew if he ever regretted being the interim superintendent of Puzzles City after S. Ringmaster left.

Dr. M. Clown - I wished I knew if she felt awkward knowing that Dr. Ringmaster told her to literally 'get rid of the weirdo'.

Mr. D. Magician - I wished I knew what did Dr. S. Ringmaster told him before I got completely beat down by his efforts to get me fired.

Mr. M. Popcorn - I wished I knew if he really understood what was happening to me that year. Only guessing but I don't expect he'd been happy about it.

Mr. R. Parade - I wished I knew why he didn't back me up when I had proven I was correct about the plan Dr. E. Strongman set that.

Mr. T. Sideshow - I wished I knew how he really felt about the awkward arrangement to have me fired even though he worked with my wife.

Ms. S. Fortune-Teller - I wished I knew what Dr. Clown told her about me and the overall plan from Dr. Ringmaster.

Ms. S. Trick-Shot - I wished I knew if she really understood the behaviors of a person who has Autism Spectrum Disorder.

Ms. A. Juggler - I wished I knew if she regretted being forced to attack me with harsh discrimination just to save her job.

Ms. A. Warrior - I wished I knew if she wanted to stay to finish the fight we had going on with the Puzzle City District.

Ms. S. Puppet - I wished I knew if she might have spoken with me today, with no legal nonsense, what would she tell me about the horrible year.

Ms. V. Acrobat - I wished I knew what she was pondering when Mr. T. Sideshow exposed her illegal venture thus turning the tables on her and what that felt like! Not pleasant, I'm sure of that! (Basically Mr. Sideshow sued V. Acrobat for misuse of school funds.)

CIRCUS RING #5

(Waiting in Line)

Chapter 13: "Different...Not Less"

I'm not the only person who worked through this silent discrimination. Many others had the same or similar experiences I had. Dr. Temple Grandin introduced us to some people in her book "Different...Not Less". (2012) One person, in particular, I needed to share was Moppy Hamilton. Moppy's occupation is a cashier at a major retail store. I can't go into much of Moppy's story but, I wanted to point out a moment in her life that is a great illustration of what I'm writing about. On page 150 in Dr. Grandin's book, she describes her experience with employment: "I hated work. I was always in trouble and got fired a lot. My parents encouraged me to work though. I even bought a car (a 1968 Rambler American that I named "Melvin"). I mostly worked in retail, but I never was a rude person or a team player, and I lost and disliked most jobs.

As I get older and I meet people with disabilities who in my opinion *could* and *should* work and would be better at it than me, I get really depressed. I can't get a doctor to medically excuse me from working, and, moneywise, I have to. I know it's bad for my health because I'm so stressed out and my feelings of how much I hate my job could give me a stroke. (She mentioned earlier in her story she was being bullied her on the job.)...I've always been stressed about being forced to coexist with people I don't choose to be with--people who are different from me...I know I do things my way, and, finally, with the help of my daughters, we told my supervisors I have Asperger's and I must be permitted to perform my job in a way that fits me without hurting the company. I feel like I can't tell everyone I'm different, and I get no respect. They just don't care." (Grandin, pg 151).

Stephen Shore is another individual Dr. Grandin introduces us to who is a fellow educator like myself. Stephen starts off talking about an accountant position he had but, he ran into problems: "After 3 months, I was let go from that position. The director of personnel said, 'Perhaps you have a disability you have not disclosed. It's not working out.' It never occurred to me at that point that difficulties I'd had with autism as a child played any role." (Grandin, pg 64) Stephen goes on the describe another work experience as a professor at a college in Boston dealing with music: "Unfortunately I lost that job, most likely because of a failure on my part to pay careful attention to office politics...While I had the support of my dean, I neglected to get an official 'OK' from a long-term faculty member from another department, who taught a single course in the music program. From that point forward, he was always at the ready to oppose future proposals of mine and eventually convinced the school to close the music department." (Grandin, pg 65)

Charli Devnet was another great example of how a boss can be considered cruel to those of us with Asperger's. Charli worked for a law firm in Atlantic City, NJ. Everything suggested is going really well for her. She had a great rapport with the secretaries, the clients, other lawyers, etc. But, then this happens: "Like many Aspies, I never saw the warning signs, which, in retrospect, I am certain were there. Perhaps my boss was growing irritated with my quirky behavior. Perhaps I was tardy once too often. Perhaps I dressed too casually in his eyes. Maybe it was not all my fault. My boss was a lone wolf himself and simply may have had no desire for a permanent associate that he had to pay week in, week out, no matter what the workload. One Friday afternoon, my boss handed me my paycheck and announced, 'This isn't working out.' I was stunned and completely blindsided." (Grandin, pg 34)

Here is some advice Dr. Temple Grandin gave from her book "The Way I See It." (2011)

"When you first meet with a prospective employer, dress neatly." (Grandin, 273)

"People respect talent. You need to be trained in an employable field, such as computer programming, drafting, or accounting." (Grandin, 274)

"You need to be punctual and show up for work on time. That also goes for being on time for scheduled meetings during office hours. Employers value dependable employees." (Grandin, 274)

"The noise and commotion of a factory or office is sometimes a problem for people with sound sensitivity. You may want to ask that your desk be located in a quieter part of the office." (Grandin, 274)

"I learned some hard lessons about being diplomatic when I had my first interactions with people at work...citing in great detail the errors in their (engineers) design and calling them 'stupid'...You simply cannot tell other people they are stupid, even if they really are stupid." (Grandin, 275)

"Being too Good." "The problem of employees jealousy is a difficult thing to understand, but it exists in the workplace...If co-workers do get jealous of your work, I found that it is helpful to try to find something they have built or done that you can genuinely compliment them on." (Grandin, 275)
"People who are polite and cheerful will have an easier time getting along at work. Make sure you always say please and thank you." (Grandin, 276)

"One of the hardest lessons I had to learn when I entered the workplace is that some people in a company had personal agendas other than doing their best work. For some, it was to climb the corporate ladder and achieve some high-level position. For others, it was to do the least amount of work possible without getting fired. Another rule I learned is to avoid discussing controversial subjects at work. Sex, religion, and political affiliations are subjects that should not be discussed at work. You can easily alienate people or give them cause to dislike you when you overstep these boundaries...Keep in mind that the 'hidden social rules' are massive and spectrum individuals usually miss most of them...Workplace politics is not easy to understand; just realize that it exists. Try to stay out of it, unless it directly jeopardizes your job or affects your ability to perform your job." (Grandin, 276-277)

I'm going to give you a couple of other people who went through the same fate as me. The first one is Robert Castleberry who had a tough battle against the system. I'm really proud that he was able to take a stand even though it had to be difficult.

A young man from Georgia who was diagnosed with Autism is suing his place of employment, the county's 4-H Youth program for not providing for his disability. "So it's Autism Spectrum Disorder, formerly Asperger's, they kind of folded Asperger's into Autism Spectrum Disorder, so it's primarily a lot of social issues," said Castleberry.

The county hired Castleberry in 2013 with an understanding of his disability but was subsequently fired in January of 2015. Which doesn't make sense if his employment already knew about his disorder.

"It (my job) was just taken from me just because I wanted some accommodations, just because I'm different," he said. I really felt exactly the same way.

You have to understand that in June of 2013 Castleberry was hired as a teacher as part of the 4-H educational programs for children.

"I could go in and I could use my creativity in the classroom and I had this 'Mr. Awesome' personality, teachers were calling me, 'Mr. Awesome,' teachers were calling me it, parents were calling me it," he said. "And I felt like I belonged and I did fit in."

In his lawsuit, Robert Castleberry said he requested simple accommodations so he could focus on his work and get away from the office noises inside the building. But, he said they were unwilling to work with him and instead they terminated his position.

"The way the offices were set up at one part of the building, the walls were literally paper-thin, you hear every conversation, every tap of keys," Castleberry said.

His firing was preceded by weeks of unrest with his managers, who eventually demanded that Castleberry see a doctor to get an official diagnosis. The demand was made in part because he had requested accommodations at his job, such as using noise-canceling headphones, avoiding office get-togethers unless mandated and taking work home to focus on his responsibilities.

Castleberry stated his "disorder" cost him the job he enjoyed; a disorder he said they requested him to disclose after telling him he must visit with one of *their* doctors to get a diagnosis.

He said it didn't stop him from thriving in the 4-H program.

The county stated Castleberry could not perform "essential" tasks of his job because it required more interaction than they believed he could handle, so they were reserved with "no choice but to fire him."

At times, the county observed how Castleberry would have a hard time contributing to meetings and often talk to himself, especially if he was scolded or corrected about some offense at work.

From the law firm of Barrett and Farahany, AJ Lakraj has been representing Castleberry from the beginning.

"Even though we are going to trial, it means Robert has to live it all over again," said Lakraj.

Lakraj says this could be a landmark case because it should set a precedent for anyone coping with Asperger's Syndrome or autistic in general.

In the judge's determination on the preliminary case, she went through both sides at length, including Castleberry's request for assistance to help with his sensitivities and his co-workers' arguments that his mannerisms made him appear "dangerous" and "defiant."

Since he was let go, Castleberry says "I haven't been able to find any employment from anyone else."

While he hopes winning the case will help him financially, Lakraj says "Robert really wants to pursue it to set an example for others who have the same disability as himself."

I'm really cheering for him because he got to do what I wished I could have done myself.

The story that broke my heart was the fate of Graham Gentles. His traumatic event was one that should NEVER have happened. In my position, I was at least given some dignity by being allowed to get my supplies and leave the building. Poor Graham got kicked out of his place of work in front of everyone, in HANDCUFFS! I remember when I first heard this story. I was furious, but then to commit suicide really hurt. This is his tragic story:

Virginia Gentles, the mother of a former Target cashier from Pasadena, California is suing the company because her son committed suicide after being disgraced by management.

The mother stated her son, 22-year-old Graham Gentles, was motivated to kill himself after he was incriminated of theft, handcuffed and in front of all of his colleagues and customers, was "paraded" through the Target store.

"He said that it was the worst day of his life because he didn't understand what was going on," said Virginia Gentles. "They humiliated him. That was their purpose!"

Graham Gentles jumped to his death from the top of a local the Courtyard Marriott, a few days after he was physically forced by store managers to take part in the ritual known as the "walk of shame."

"The intention of the policy is to humiliate and shame, and in this particular instance the policy had its intended effect with tragic results," said attorney Patrick McNicholas.

The lawsuit sites false imprisonment, wrongful negligence and purposeful infliction of emotional damage.

According to the mother, Graham Gentles was pulled in by police and Target security personnel at the entrance of the store as he came to work.

The suit states that police forcefully restrained him, emptied the contents in his pockets and ripped his hat off. In the direction of two members of the store management, he was handcuffed and led to an office, according to the deposition.

"Gentles was shocked, confused and mortified at being handcuffed and walked through the Target store in front of co-workers and store customers. Mr. Gentles had no idea why he was being arrested," the lawyer stated.

Graham Gentles was wheeled off to the police station, but he was let go the same day with no charges filed.

Mr. Nicholas, the lawyer for the mother said Gentles, who had Asperger's Syndrome, "experienced severe emotional distress" following the altercation.

"He said, 'Mom, I've never stolen,'" Virginia Gentles recalled. "He said, 'They did the walk of shame, I had to do the walk of shame. But they only do that when people steal and I've never stolen a thing.'"

"This was part of his extended family," added McNicholas. "He had indicated that he felt safe there. This is where his friends were, so he felt as though he lost all of that in one moment."

The suit alleges that a disagreement between Graham Gentles and a fellow worker at a tavern outside of work may have ignited the argument. The complaint says it's understood that claims made by the fellow worker led to the decision of store management to call for Gentles' arrest and "walk of shame."

According to the Target personnel, the so-called "walk of shame" has happened on numerous occasions to employees who were suspected of stealing.

"One of the primary purposes of this lawsuit is that Target stops the policy immediately [and] recognizes the harm that it could do," said McNicholas.

Target released a statement, saying, "Our thoughts and sympathies go out to the friends and family of this individual. The allegations in the lawsuit of a Target policy or practice are simply not true. There is no such policy. As this is pending litigation, we don't have further comment at this time."

"The nature of Asperger's Graham tended to be hyper-focus and so he was very hyper-focused on this," McNicholas said. "He was hyper-focused on his loss and it was a perfect storm which resulted in his death."

I've heard many more examples of working people with Autism Spectrum Disorder who had struggled with the same fate as these other people and myself. Even other members of my family have dealt with the Silent Discrimination directly. I consider this ignored issue serious. Yes, we celebrate Autism Awareness for the full month of April, but I really wonder if the awareness is happening especially in the job force. We can't go on pretending that this isn't a problem. Real people with this disability have mostly been facing these challenges all their lives. Many times, people with ASD may not understand why they were terminated or not rehired solely based on their condition. Employers have a way of finding any stupid excuse to remove all the weirdos because they're different and the boss' expectations never meet their level because it's not done the way they want it.

Education is key. The workforce needs to understand that we are not all equally created; the Silent Discrimination cannot continue. Lives are being ruined or worse... lost. All of you with Autism Spectrum Disorder, you need to recognize your rights; you have them and don't let it go to waste. We only have one life; you deserve to live it the way you want.

"If there is no ***fight***, there is no ***change***."

Chapter 14: Trying To Change The Rules

There are always two sides to one story. Professions try their best to help the general public be informed on any changes that happen in our society. One polarizing part of our medical field is mental health. As I've described earlier in this book, having other adults being able to understand those of us with these mental conditions is always a constant battle. The only thing that could really throw the comprehension for people who don't understand different mental condition is if the 'professionals' decide to complete redefine everything. Sadly, that did that very thing with the newest Diagnostic and Statistical Manual of Mental Disorders also known as DSM-5. This book was released in 2013 and now everyone is confused.

Having the American Psychiatric Association decide to place people with Asperger's Syndrome in the general autism category was thought to be bad, well this is now worse. They have decided to divide the different personality disabilities under "clusters". I will say some of these will not be a big surprise while there are others that make no sense what so ever. The definitions for each disability did not really change but, the placement did raise eyebrows. I will be looking at each cluster to define and argue the points of these groupings. I will the finalize my opinion based on their observations and why this can make things worse.

Cluster **A** consists of Paranoid Personality Disorders, Schizoid Personality Disorders, and Schizotypal Personality Disorder. The DSM-5 describes **A** as individuals with these often appear off or erratic. They believe 5.7% of these people fall into this cluster. Here is where one would find those who have schizophrenia, bipolar disorder and depressive disorders. The description of cluster **A** is found on page 649 (APA, 2013) in the DSM-5 book. My only thought on this is wouldn't a paranoid disorder be more of a neurological disability? I do want to note that bipolar disorder falls under this cluster. The reason I point this out is because people who are misdiagnosed with autism actually have this disorder because in a small way they tend to mirror similar traits. I don't want to go into detail about each these disorders but, I sort of agree that this is an appropriate class or cluster they can be placed in but, I can't help wonder if their definition is correct.

Cluster **B** consists of Antisocial Personality Disorder, Borderline Personality Disorder, Histrionic Personality Disorder, and Narcissistic Personality Disorder. The DSM-5 describes **B** as individuals with these disorders often appear dramatic, emotional, or erratic. They believe 1.5% of these people fall into this cluster. They state that the pattern seems to follow a psychopathy, sociopathy or dissocial personality disorder. The description of cluster **B** is found on page 659 (APA 2013) in the DSM-5 book. The one that draws quite a bit of criticism is the Narcissistic Personality Disorder. The reasons are simple it's generally looked upon as a 'normal' trait the only issue is that condition being greatly overt or grandiose for people who have this issue. There is treatment for this condition but, I wonder if there is a simpler way of addressing this 'disorder' because I do have a hard time wrapping my head around the idea that narcissism is a mental issue. The argument can be made if this condition is one of those nature versus nurture. Was the person born this way or was the condition a learned experience growing up?

Cluster **C** consists of Avoidant Personality Disorder, Dependent Personality Disorder and Obsessive-Compulsive Personality Disorder. The DSM-5 describe **C** as individuals with these disorders often appear anxious or fearful. They believe 6.0% of these people fall in to this cluster. They state that the pattern is a pervasive one of social inhibition, feelings of inadequacy, and hypersensitivity to negative evaluation that begins by early adulthood and is present in a variety of contexts. The description of cluster **C** is found on page 672 (APA, 2013) in the DSM-5 book. The only thing that comes to my mind is these tend to be a few of the symptoms that those who are autistic. I've mentioned how I have OCD but, I deal with depression as well. See, this can get rather confusing and sometimes you might leave the doctor's office more unsure than when you walked in. Again, I don't want to do into detail about this because the grouping seems appropriate for this issue because I've already spoken on this since I have this condition myself.

The professionals do admit that the clustering system has serious limitations and has not been consistently validated. Before the clusters, the professionals do point out the 'general personality disorders like bipolar, depression, anxiety, PTSD, substance disorders, anything that deals with a head trauma. I'm sure your question is – "Where is autism?" They decided to classify this in a completely separate category…Neurodevelopment Disorders. If you're wondering about the term "Asperger's" this is what the book notes – "Individuals with a well-established DSM-IV diagnosis of autistic disorder, Asperger's disorder, or pervasive developmental disorder not otherwise specified should be given the diagnosis of autism spectrum. [Meaning, the term Asperger's is being thrown out.] Individuals who have marked deficits in social communication, but whose symptoms do not otherwise meet criteria for autism spectrum disorder, should be evaluated for social (pragmatic) communication disorder." (APA, 2013, page 51) This quote that I just shared is the ONLY time the word Asperger's is mentioned in the entire book! I will say that the DSM-5 does break down the severity level of those who are on the autism spectrum. There are three levels altogether.

The severity levels are labeled as 'Requiring **very** substantial support' [Level 3], 'Requiring substantial support' [Level 2] and 'Requiring support' [Level 1]. From this point, they divided the three levels with two columns. One deals with 'Social communication' and the second is 'Restricted, repetitive behaviors. So, for a person who would fall on the first level, their social communication might have a hard time initiating any kind of social discussion and would lack interest in social settings. For the restricted behavior, this might include having a hard time changing up activities or not being able to organize themselves. On the second level, communication becomes more difficult where they might only speak in simple sentences and their nonverbal movements could be off from the message they are trying to convey. Restricted, the second level can't cope with change and might even cause distress. The final third level, communication skills would be very limited with little intellectual understanding or minimal response to others. For restrictions, the third can't deal change at all with a high level of distress and focus.

All of the clusters were placed under the Personality Disorders and this makes some sense. We'll get the personality disorders due to the neurodevelopment but, the personality disorders were supposed to be formed through other means. I've been reading several comments on-line in which people are trying to tie together neurodevelopment with personality disorders and these two things really need to have their own distinction because I believe this can be a little dangerous. Lumping the two complete different disorders can cause a great deal of misinformation. The only other thing that disturbs me is with all of these classifications, I have to argue the idea of...what is normal? If we are going to keep throwing on more mental issues and it seems at times, 'phantom disorders', where is this going to end? Are we doing this for the right reasons?

I did state earlier that I feel Asperger's has been over diagnosed on too many occasions. I know you're asking me how I make this claim, I see it in my schools. I teach Special Education and I really do have Asperger's. When I learn that another child had been diagnosed, I'll do my own test to see if this is really true. A few times the child really is autistic and in others, they are not. I believe mental health is important in helping each person with the problem, the question should be – Do they really have one? I will question the money trail of this one. In the end, pharmaceutical companies are counting on more people to get their medication that was treat...whatever ails them. The worst part is that this sadly makes too much sense. Doctors seem to have plenty samples for people and if there is something 'wrong' then let's find a pill to fix it. Mental Health or otherwise any issue they can cure. We need to step back to take a harder look or this will end up like another circus.

REFERENCES

American Psychiatric Association. (2013) *Diagnostic and Statistical Manual of Mental Disorders*. Fifth Edition. Arlington, VA: American Psychiatric Association.

Grandin, T. (2012) *Different...Not Less*. Arlington, Texas: Future Horizons. Pgs. 34, 64-65, 150-151

Grandin, T. (2011) *The Way I See it*. Arlington, Texas: Future Horizons. Pgs. 273-277

EPILOGUE

 I wanted to mention that I recently discovered a fairly new condition that I didn't have before until now. After going through several physical episodes in my body, I wasn't sure what was happening to me. I learned that I now suffer from Panic Attacks. Like many of you, I thought this was some silly little feeling you get like just before you're getting on a scary rollercoaster. I was wrong. On WebMD, they describe a panic attack like this:

Panic attacks involve sudden feelings of terror that strike without warning. These episodes can occur at any time, even during sleep. People experiencing a panic attack may believe they are having a heart attack or they are dying or going crazy. The fear and terror that a person experiences during a panic attack are not in proportion to the true situation and may be unrelated to what is happening around them. Most people with panic attacks experience several of the following symptoms:

"Racing" heart

Feeling weak, faint, or dizzy

Tingling or numbness in the hands and fingers

Sense of terror or impending doom or death

Feeling sweaty or having chills

Chest pains

Breathing difficulties

Feeling a loss of control

Panic attacks generally last longer than 10 minutes, although some symptoms may persist for a much longer time. People who have had one panic attack are at greater risk for having subsequent panic attacks than those who have never experienced a panic attack. When the attacks occur repeatedly, and there is worry about having more episodes, they consider a person to have a condition known as panic disorder.

When Does Worry Turn into Anxiety That Needs Treatment?

When worrying interferes with your daily life, then you should seek professional help.

People with panic disorder may be extremely anxious and fearful since they cannot predict when the next episode will occur. Panic disorder is fairly common and affects about 6 million adults in the U.S. Women are twice as likely as men to develop the condition, and its symptoms usually begin in early adulthood.

It is not clear what causes the panic disorder. In many people who have the biological vulnerability to panic attacks, they may develop in association with major life changes (such as getting married, having a child, starting the first job, etc.) and major lifestyle stressors. There is also some evidence that suggests that the tendency to develop panic disorder may run in families. People who suffer from panic disorder are also more likely than others to suffer from depression, attempt suicide, or to abuse alcohol or drugs.

Fortunately, panic disorder is a treatable condition. Psychotherapy and medications have both been used, either singly or in combination, for the successful treatment of panic disorder. If medication is necessary, your doctor may prescribe anti-anxiety medications, certain antidepressants or sometimes certain anticonvulsant drugs that also have anti-anxiety properties, or a class of heart medications known as beta-blockers to help prevent or control the episodes in panic disorder.

This is no joke. I suffer through these and I am now seeking treatment myself. If you have these similar symptoms. Please go visit your doctor right away.

COLOR ME!!! Who says you can't have a little fun with a book? Feel free to put some color to Paolo the Puzzle Parrot! (But you wouldn't expect this from a *Weirdo*... Right?)

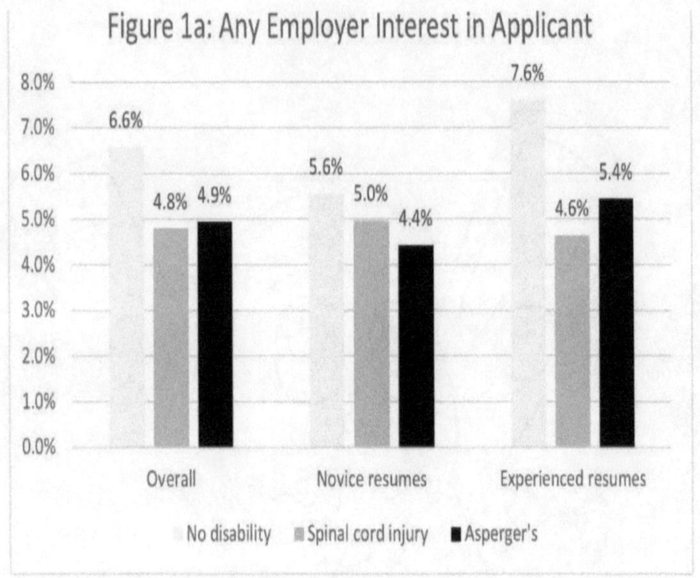

National Bureau of Economic Research

Here is the reality of those of us who are autistic and are looking for employment.

Other books by the same author:

Be An Autism Avenger

Pieces Left Behind

Darcy's Run

Starring Down Annihilation